for Charles Hood

with good wishes —
after the 3.9 quake
in Irvine, Ca —

Edwin Haig

Feb. 27, 1984.

POETS NOW

Edited by Robert Peters

1. *Jonathan Williams*, Get Hot or Get Out
2. *Rochelle Ratner*, Practicing To Be A Woman
3. *Jerry Ratch*, Hot Weather
4. *David Ray*, The Touched Life
5. *Carolyn Stoloff*, A Spool of Blue
6. *Edwin Honig*, Interrupted Praise

INTER-
RUPTED
PRAISE

*New and Selected Poems
by Edwin Honig*

Poets Now 6

The Scarecrow Press, Inc.
Metuchen, N.J., & London 1983

BOOKS BY EDWIN HONIG

Poetry
THE MORAL CIRCUS, Contemporary Library Series, 1955
THE GAZABOS: FORTY-ONE POEMS, Clarke & Way, 1959; augmented ed., 1961
POEMS FOR CHARLOTTE, Clarke & Way, 1963
SURVIVALS, October House, 1964
SPRING JOURNALS: POEMS, Wesleyan University Press, 1968
FOUR SPRINGS, Swallow Press, 1972
AT SIXES, Burning Deck Press, 1974
SHAKE A SPEAR WITH ME, JOHN BERRYMAN, Copper Beech Press, 1974
THE AFFINITIES OF ORPHEUS, Copper Beech Press, 1976
SELECTED POEMS (1955–1976), Texas Center for Writers Press, 1979

Prose
GARCIA LORCA, New Directions, 1944, 1963; Octagon Books, 1981
DARK CONCEIT: THE MAKING OF ALLEGORY, Northwestern University Press, 1959; Faber & Faber, 1960; Oxford University Press, 1966; Brown University Press, 1972
CALDERON AND THE SEIZURES OF HONOR, Harvard University Press, 1972
THE FOIBLES AND FABLES OF AN ABSTRACT MAN, Copper Beech Press, 1980

Plays
THE WIDOW: A VERSE PLAY IN ONE ACT, in *The Gazabos,* augmented ed., 1961
ORPHEUS BELOW, in *The Affinities of Orpheus,* 1976
CALISTO AND MELIBEA, Hellcoal Press, 1972

Translations
CALDERON: FOUR PLAYS, Hill & Wang, 1961
INTERLUDES: CERVANTES, New American Library, 1964
LIFE IS A DREAM: A PLAY BY PEDRO CALDERON DE LA BARCA, Hill & Wang, 1970
SELECTED POEMS OF FERNANDO PESSOA, Swallow Press, 1971
DIVAN AND OTHER WRITINGS BY FEDERICO GARCIA LORCA, Copper Beech Press, 1977

Library of Congress Cataloging in Publication Data

Honig, Edwin.
 Interrupted praise: New and Selected Poems.

 (Poets now; 6)
 I. Title. II. Series.
 PS3515.O49915   1983   811'.52   82-5998
 ISBN 0-8108-1564-8   AACR2

Copyright © 1983 by Edwin Honig
Manufactured in the United States of America

To Milton Miller

What you went to find wasn't there.
But out of the fire into empty air
A child sings back the panicky thirties,
And the snub-tailed barber snips your hair.

ACKNOWLEDGMENTS

The author wishes to thank the editors of the following periodicals, in which some of these poems first appeared: *Accent, Audience, Audit, Beloit Poetry Journal, Boston Phoenix, Boston University Journal, Burning Deck, Chelsea, Colorado Quarterly, Commonweal, English Leaflets, Furioso, Here and Now, Images, Kenyon Review, Michigan Quarterly Review, Mutiny, New Boston Review, New Directions Annual, The Nation, New Mexico Quarterly, New Republic, New York Quarterly, New York Times, The New Yorker, Poetry, Poetry Now, The Saturday Review, Southwest Review, Virginia Quarterly Review, Voices, Western Review, Yankee.*

Previously published books from which poems in this volume appear are: The Moral Circus, copyright © 1955 by Edwin Honig; *The Gazabos: 41 Poems and The Widow,* copyright © 1959, 1961 by Edwin Honig; *Survivals,* copyright © 1955, 1959, 1961, 1964 by Edwin Honig; *Spring Journal,* copyright © 1960, 1963, 1967, 1968, by Edwin Honig; *Four Springs,* copyright © 1967, 1968, 1972 by Edwin Honig; *At Sixes,* copyright © 1974 by Edwin Honig; *The Affinities of Orpheus,* copyright © 1972, 1974, 1976 by Edwin Honig; *Selected Poems (1955–1976),* copyright © 1979 by Edwin Honig.

INTRODUCTION

For *Interrupted Praise,* Edwin Honig has assembled work written over a forty-year period. Roughly half of this volume was published in a *Selected Poems* (1979), under the imprint of the Texas Center for Writers Press. This book is now out of print. The presence of so much new work in this current volume attests to Honig's undiminished vigor. We are privileged to include him among the first in the Poets Now series.

In arranging his new collection, Honig departs from convention by presenting his newest work first, later moving back in time. What a refreshing design! In the 13 September 1979 issue of *East Side–West Side,* a tabloid published in Providence, the poet talks about experiences that influenced his becoming a writer. The first event, one that has haunted him all his life and is the theme of a recent poem, was the accidental death of a younger brother, when Honig was five. Also, there was another experience, a "nearly fatal bout with nephritis," when he was nine. He then continues with some "positive" influences: "my illiterate grandmother, who spoke Spanish, Arabic, and Yiddish (but no English); I lived with her and my grandfather for a few years after my parents were divorced when I was twelve. Experiences of this sort urged certain necessities upon me: one was to write instead of choking; another, to make sense of the world around me—but sense that would not be bereft of my own fantasy. Both my poetry and my criticism seem to rise out of such a need: the criticism that creates . . . and the poetry that criticizes persons and places I have loved and distrusted—'moral circuses' and 'gazabos'—." Other literary achievements he alludes to are his translations of Calderón, Pessoa, Lope de Vega, Miguel Hernández, and Lorca. He has also written plays and seminal books on Lorca, on allegory, and on the theme of honor in Calderónian tragedy.

The drift in Honig's work over the years is toward an increased clarity of statement and image. He no longer seems to feel the need to prove that part of his inventiveness is an ability to wield the surreal, metaphysical, or decorative image. "For an Immigrant Grandmother," 1955, reveals his early techniques. In these opening lines, the simple fact of the woman's zest for life is encrusted with imagery:

> She sat for an age at the window with glances that threw
> Pennies of pity at collarless beggars, and cripples
> Who crawled like crabs from gutter to curb rippled
> The geese in the bag of her hunched-over flesh. But you
> Always could tell by her murmur for heaven to witness
> When neighborhood children like sparrows hopped in distress
> To catch from the hand of the baker his three-day-old bread.

This is a poetry, excellent in its kind, reflecting the complex style Honig had absorbed, probably from his readings in Spanish and English poetry. It is typically derived from models that young poets were reading and revering in post–World War II America: Pound, Eliot, Yeats, and Stevens, poets who preferred a private, even esoteric poetry to an easily graspable, more public work.

When we examine the first poem of "To Restore a Dead Child," the sequence that opens *Interrupted Praise,* we see differences. Honig's voice is clearer now, the images are more direct and experiental, and the language lacks any self-conscious brilliance:

1925

Sometimes while I sleep
I hear the single cry and tire screek
that never end.
My blond and foolish brown-eyed brother
lugging his fretful love
shambles after me
as the cunning Mack truck
lurching out of nowhere
cuts him down.

He's a long dead almost-three.
I'm a long lived five
just turned sixty-one
still running in a dead heat

with the rolling cab that swooped him up
heading for the vanished hospital.

It's then on waking
I feel the snot of infant faces
leak into my mouth.

All this is incredibly stark and unforgettable. Despite the interval of fifty-six years, the event rings as harrowingly as if it had just occurred. Yet, despite this directness, Honig never writes as if he were fashioning the newspaper of his life for half-alert readers to scan over their morning coffee. For the Honig of the fifties remains secure in the Honig of the eighties. Although the imagery is less otiose, the craftsmanship continues impeccable.

For Honig, the poem has always been a well-crafted form in which intelligence, control, and invention merge and balance. He is skilled both at free verse and traditional forms. He exalts the creative function above the purely inspirational—the latter evident in poems by writers who simply open sluices of feelings and let them flow. Obviously, in "To Restore a Dead Child," Honig's pain is harrowing; to live with such guilt, despite one's innocence, remains a fact as omnipresent as the breaking of one's daily bread. Yet Honig manipulates the tone of the piece with such skill that sentimentality, that scabrous monster, remains at bay. The tough, direct words *screek* and *snot* are potent; and Honig's fashioning of a lighter tone via *blond and foolish, cunning,* and *swooped* contrast with the severity of the tragedy.

While these two poems, one early and one late, reflect stylistic perimeters of sorts, and prepare readers unacquainted with Honig's work for what they will find, they should not be read as evidence of severe ruptures or shifts. What impresses, in fact, is a remarkable continuity of theme throughout. Two major motifs, for example, unify the poems: nature and house.

Honig's poet is usually a solitary man, even when he is in love. His deployment of the self as a prototypical human displaced, questing for love and affection in the midst of vast frustrations, he projects against nature. He walks into "the woods of pain" to find release; and he moves into areas of dune and forest to locate the detachment he needs for sorting out his imaginative life—a continuing process. His long series on "Spring" is among the best long nature poems of its time. The older poet's wanderings toward more isolation may symbolize an easing into his own death, which he seems to imply will be a kind of vaporizing into a universal natural flux. Always, even as a young poet, isolation was a central fact in his life; and from it came the poetry, and its indulgence in the metaphysical and speculative—the themes of seed, life, growth, death—everywhere in these poems. "We give birth to ourselves," he writes, "on the brink of dying." Other souls, not yet born, "shudder and ogle" as we stumble and dance toward our own "negligible" passing.

The *house,* a symbol of the protective shells we fashion for our lives, is ubiquitous here. At times, the poet stands outside his house looking in at those sleeping there. At other times, he is inside writing and meditating. In "The Island" (1964) he sits indoors, at 2 a.m., writing about the meanings of house/room to his art and life. Only partial fulfillment and release from cravings result; a cryptic, bothersome force continues to wait hidden behind the window sash, wanting in:

> This is the room with books and chairs
> that waits inaudibly; what does
> the silence not-a-silence ask?
> It asks the breath, the useful eyes
> that scan it uselessly, what lives.
> It asks to be, and not be listened
> to; unmoved, unused, unkept,
> waiting and awaited,
> it begins an aftermath.
>
> What knocks behind the sash knows this,
> knows what least there is to know, to be.
> Always he craves to enter, knowing,
> as he did this room tonight, waiting
> to begin the waiting afterward,
> sharing—safe, estranged—the silence
> of a room, an envelope,
> a feeble knocking at the sash,
> shared past death beyond the aftermath.

In "Dialogue in the Sleeping House (c. 1976), the image recurs, intensifying the self-isolation and detachment so natural to Honig. Here, though, the connection with death implied earlier in "The Island" moves to an easeful threnody:

deep through the windows

> *because to exist a wish needs*
> *detachment from what feeds it*

as to engrave its light

> *the possibility to continue detached*
> *is probably almost infinite*

in the sleeping house forever.

In this too-brief introduction, I have suggested merely a few ways of entering Honig's poems—and there are others that sensitive readers will soon discern. Honig informs us ("To Restore a Dead Child: #8) that in *Interrupted Praise* we may appear to be reading about his vague shadows—but in truth we are not: the *form* is more *his* than is "our idea of him." As we perceive and feel him in these remarkable poems (and a number are in the voices of personae), we see "the dark loose patches / fallen from him in the light." And, if we are able, as we assemble our envisionings and impressions into a whole, we will do so because those very patches, even after their author's death, will keep "trying to fill and fill / all that was left / of his living clothes / before his body vanished." The energies of the poet will continue as living charges after the poet's demise. I am sure that readers will find *Interrupted Praise* a remarkably whole cloth; we expect that Edwin Honig will continue for years to spin more of it. He is at the top of his powers.

Robert Peters
Editor, *Poets Now*

CONTENTS

1. Poems 1980–1981

To Restore a Dead Child

1. 1925	3
2. Hearing it wake, we feel	4
3. We walked out of time	5
4. Watching the immense self scattering ocean	6
5. For everyone the call of light	7
6. As we would have it	8
7. Not to be listening	9
8. As the light descended	10
9. No longer would he have to run	11

The Abstract Man Encounters the Adjutant

1. Echoing the fierce belief that time	12
2. In his ordinary world	13
3. The isolated house he sometimes visited	14
4. In winter when the sun shone	15
5. There would be large cuttings of flowers	16
6. Suddenly out of the hedge	17
7. The grave thumps	18

Soldier   19

By Sea Stone

1. Blackening ebbtide   20
2. These stones if they spoke   21
3. Nothing much left   21
4. Can you remember beginning   22
5. All the nights the house slept through   23
6. Conrad saw behind the wheel   24
7. To be alive be bold   25

Teetering   26

2. Poems 1976–1980

Promise   29
After the Letter   30
Listen   32
Being Somebody   33
Letter from New Hampshire   37
An Art of Summer   40
Starting the Hostilities   44
Passionflower   45
Opening   46
I Need You   47
After the Separation   48
The House   49
Monster Talk   51
Dialogue in the Sleeping House   52
Without Love   53
Passes for Nicanor Parra   54

xiii

Partita	55
The Painter in the Mountain	56
For His Mother Flying into Her Seventy-seventh	57
Stumbling Out of the Prado	58
Rilke's White Horse	58
Another March	59
Come	60
Night Island	61
Sweeping the Room	62
Last Song	62
G. W. M.	63
Pablo Neruda	64
Three Moments for George Sullivan	65

3. The Affinities of Orpheus

Through You	73
His Dream	73
His Chain	74
Another	74
A Wind Dies	75
Melting Song	76
Another Orpheus	77
Joy: An End Song	78
Lines for Dancers	79
Who	81

4. Four Springs

From *Spring One*
1. Suffused by paint-cracking warmth in a steam-heated room 87

4. The President stands up to hundreds
    of millions, a dog   87
8. I find a man sitting inside myself
    and leering   88
17. Brute, wise man, ogre, and beauty,
    cripple and President   89
19. As spring comes back each year with
    its new work and cares   90
22. High noon. It's time to get up—
    jump into my pants   91

From *Spring Two*
1. The days are gentler, frosts are paper
    thin   91
2. In one I see a man sitting way
    beyond me   92
7. How was it in childhood almost to
    have died?   93
8. It was to live   93
9. It was lifelong to be his only
    brother's death   94
18. Coming back from New York on the
    New Haven Line, the day   96

From *Spring Three*
3. A woman plays life   99

From *Spring Four*
1. The interminable colors of life   100
5. The papers say six chairs around a
    table   101
6. The world is changing as we think
    it   102
7. Tomorrow will happen   102

12. I follow my words like an ant on his
    pile   102
13. My heart is a love that I like and
    dislike   103

5. Spring Journal: Poems

The Dead   107
Her Hand   107
For Margot   109
Birth Song: In the Wing Seat, at Night   110
Second Son Day   114
Nativity   115
Race   116
November Through a Giant Copper Beech   117
Bodega, Goodbye   119

6. Survivals

Tête à Tête   123
Glad Day   123
The Island   124
The Weather's Criminal   130
The Furnace   135
It Cannot Be It Is   137
For C.   138
Wife   138
My Love Is Asleep   139
What Changes, My Love   140
Death with Its Cup of Hopefulness   141
Unless Love Die   141

Passing	142
Now, Before the End, I Think	143
Now, My Usefulness Over	144

7. The Gazabos: Forty-one Poems

Happening	149
Island Storm	149
Speech	151
Quest	152
The Tall Toms	152
As a Great Prince	153
May 1945	154
Jane Retreat	154
Ancestors	155
For an Immigrant Grandmother	156
Grammarian Thumbing an Old Text	157
Lease and Loss	158
The Marriage	159
Outer Drive	159
Walt Whitman	160
The Gazabos	162

8. The Moral Circus

Last Act	167
Hamlet	168
The Moral Circus	169
"Do You Love Me?"	170
Ditty to His Love	172
First Morning	173

POEMS 1980–1981

TO RESTORE A DEAD CHILD

1

1925

Sometimes while I sleep
I hear the single cry and tire screek
that never end.
My blond and foolish brown-eyed brother
lugging his fretful love
shambles after me
as the cunning Mack truck
lurching out of nowhere
cuts him down.

He's a long dead almost-three.
I'm a long lived five
just turned sixty-one
still running in a dead heat
with the rolling cab that swooped him up
heading for the vanished hospital.

It's then on waking
I feel the snot of infant faces
leak into my mouth.

2

Hearing it wake, we feel
the windy calling to each other
of the kindred sleep and death
in the morning opening
of the eyes of country horses,
the odor of earth's dampness
in the crystal tree light,
and the touch of rough bark
on fingertips.

Seeing it, we feel again
the worn heart welcoming
the slow envelopment of dark,
the falling off of sight
in the old gray house,
when sun's heat passes
and the first breeze
lifts a faint dust
along the hedges.

Remembering, again we see
the embers crumbling in the grate,
the fire flaring up again,
the pause before the turning shadow
spans the polished floor
and drifts into the open world,
a street that wanders
endless as a silent grief
that will never know itself.

3

We walked out of time
into the woods of pain
and never seemed
the same again.
We tilted with the hope
of finding ourself
in another skin,
and bent on recovering,
turned with open eyes
to find welcome in the arms
of a dead brother—
sleeping his dream of being,
a dream so long unfulfilled
there was no time
even to begin to live it,
till in his own hope
we lived what we believed
may have been
reserved for him.

4

Watching the immense self scattering ocean
ruffle out before us,
our wonder stirred and time became
an intricately formal mating,
night on day on night,
a repeated wave flash
signaling the act and its abating,
and the last long rolling into shore
turned into a fresh aspiring
of newborn creatures
to join the greater mating
sky and ocean,
and the creatures reeling beyond our wonder
mingled with the lifetimes
of our aged parents, each one apart,
our cheerful sister's pregnant daughter,
also apart,
and this briefly sunlit reawakening
stung alive the still unanswered
·black and blueness
we never would be clear of—
though no longer cherishing
the old bruised core,
no longer poised against
the battering disablements,
we simply gazed again
and let our wonder live again,
and die.

5

For everyone the call of light,
seeing figures of the creatures
from the mountain and the sea:
an eagle flying and a snake
whipping past the chicken coop,
a horse neighing in a flash
of meadow, with wayward water there
to slake the thirst a moment.
As light descends,
following the slow shapes
bulking briefly in their place,
it makes as if to stop
and give them way and cause,
as if to stroke
and praise their substance fully
before each creature
passes into its own remove
with rapid smile print
(as on your face and mine appears
held there by heads soon to be
no longer yours or mine)
till it lets the shadow quicken,
overtake the bobbing bulks,
and rise immensely over
like a mercy to devour them.

6

As we would have it,
it would be nothing simple
or profound,
nothing easily attained,
long worked for or perfected.
It would be of a wholeness,
full and large and figured
in its substance.
It would be all engrossing
to itself and others—
like the playing of a mindless tune
between a richer music
and a silence:
a peaked and dribbling sound,
a sound wavering in descent
but kept in measure,
and in that measure
letting all know
how deeply it could love
the silence following.

7

Not to be listening
yet to be heard
in the huge inconsequences
of the heart,
where having conveyed
the full measure of our hate
as a gesture of belief
in something worse than ourself
is barely to have escaped
self murder,
the intended sacrifice
become the bound body of love
in a younger self—
wearing a brother's features
still scored through
the dead boy's memory—
forever jammed between
the tonnage of his death
and self hate's last convulsions,
like the lost deserter
fixed in an ice cake
some intruder yells up
early one spring.

8

As the light descended
the night was pierced a moment
and there was seen
in the vagueness of a shadow
a form more his
than our idea of him,
and the shadow wobbled
into a figure merging
with the hope of his lost being
come to be again,
as we tried swiftly to put on
the dark loose patches
fallen from him in the light—
trying to fill and fill
all that was left
of his living clothes
before his body vanished.

9

No longer would he have to run
each time we left him
before our mindless going
struck him
as needing to be answered,
and the need make him
fly to us
and press his body
on us briefly.

For now, if again we left
without a smile or hand wave,
he would no longer need to fret
or wonder how to weight the meaning
since as last reminder
he had left
his body printed on us.

THE ABSTRACT MAN ENCOUNTERS THE ADJUTANT

1

Echoing the fierce belief that time
serves only as a part-time adjutant,
he lost each battle he ever deigned to fight,
construing every language
but the adjutant's outspokenness.

So it came to pass he had
no prospects, no supports,
except for those he chose to think
would be revealed when needed,
as if he'd summoned them.

His secret hope was that the adjutant,
who lived for others and for none,
would one day touch his eyes
so he could read the real language
things were written in.

2

In his ordinary world
past and future did not exist
except if he decided
they should appear
peopled with events,
with casual births and deaths,
minute misfortunes of any kind,
but where his own hopes and desires
played no part.

As long as he directed it,
this play assigned the present
to the adjutant miming his way
through muffed contingencies,
the arch reflector of everything
flowing past his eyes.

And so he stood reflecting
as if to ask, how could one
who chose to focus on
the landscape of the livid moment,
observing life so keenly,
be said to have no heart, or worse,
not to be alive?

3

The isolated house he sometimes visited
had the virtue of facing ocean
from every door and window.
No sign of people anywhere.
A few gulls here and there, and other birds
he had no wish to name.
Occasionally a ship
appeared to fill the sky—
but diminished if he stared,
shrank further if he glanced away,
then vanished utterly.

He discovered that
since things appear
to disappear so swiftly,
they had no need for names.
Suppose he asked, What's that?
and he replied, Possibly a crab—
it would seem he'd thrown
a loose stocking over it, making
the whole thing wrinkle right away.

Better to answer silence with silence.
Each thing moving apart,
no thing needed his speech.
This gave him a certain satisfaction.

4

In winter when the sun shone,
winds sometimes descended
in a ritual drumming up of clouds,
which in fact filed by,
peered quickly down
and crossed the sky, to be devoured
by whatever lay in wait
past the horizon.

Meanwhile in town
a mother cat had a litter
and out of spite or hunger
ate the kittens one by one
as soon as they emerged
from her mysterious dark hole.

5

There would be large cuttings of flowers
where he walked, left at intervals
in heavy piles, as though the same rough hand
that cut the stems
must soon return to gather everything
in one huge wicker basket
centered in a noiseless cart.
Conveyed into the house beyond
to gaze from cut-glass bowls
and pots of blue majolica,
the flowers would at last appear
expertly propped, consummately transformed.

But the adjutant delayed or never came,
the flowers wilted,
hailstones clattered angrily,
and every door leading to the house
kept banging in the wind.

6

Suddenly out of the hedge
a rabbit leaps clear,
scampers past the bread crumbs
laid out for the mourning dove,
and almost transparently
disappears through an opening
to the rocks below.

The dawn is pondering
how to put out
the sheerest sickle moon
as a flock of geese
makes a quick signature
across the brimming cold waters.

Day with its swift demands
will soon leach light
out of every object
in its defiant shapeliness
and crystal visibility.

It is precisely then
the adjutant begins to tell.

7

The grave thumps
and the upward thought leaps to uncover ground
where the last idea
of the downborne man was sunk.

See how pure the man reborn of inklings
now appears with his new umbilicus
forged link by link
from relatives of happiness
crying *Jubilee of jubilees,*
I was, therefore I think.

SOLDIER

I did not die in that war
or in any war quite
though I died in the first
and all the wars since—
at first all at once
then with practice
a bit at a time

While I'm alive
I'm ready to die any day
in a war—
the value of dying
is in daring
to come back

If I die in the next
as I did in the first
you who survive
might understand
it was good for something
though not wanting
necessarily
to applaud me—
and I wouldn't blame you
much as I'd envy
your being alive

So I'd have to come back
because you'd forget
no matter how many times
you'd read it all in the papers—

*he's so good at dying
he died in the Punics
War II the Crusades
poor bastard can't stop
he's at it again*

BY SEA STONE

1

Blackening ebbtide
      sings dumbly by you
whipped by a wind swirl
      weed hair drips over
stone bodies huddled
      in monkish communion
making low song
      of unshaken risings
and dim withdrawals
      of long breathing waters

2

These stones if they spoke
could tell what lives—
one doubled flowing

an outgone returning
of timed open sea
conveying a smallness

like breath in the air
drawn out and in
of a hugeness—

ends as a slippage
of stone upon stone
on a packed sea shelf

3

Nothing much left
to stop your breathing,
you still swim out
and the waves topple you
arriving back.

All those green eyes
littering the beach—

the glinting lovers
and their surviving wives,
no longer lovers,
of dead friends—
stare past you at routs
of winter starlings overhead,
disregarding trophies.

Mozart hums the distance
out to sea and back.
Poised and never waiting,
the red sun pricks your eyelids—
take heart
        take heart . . .
You love your heart
even when it falls
and is not dead.

4

Can you remember beginning
to shape your solitude?
Was it clarity or fog
that started it?

Maybe the eye caught by a rose
tore on a thorn, and the moon,

peculiarly close, hung bleeding
till you could almost bear it.

To be flesh of the thing that felt
the pangs of its beginning
is only to know you must trace
the end inside of you.

Now and then you hear
a window frozen
in its frame creaking
as if the moon was back.

5

All the nights the house slept through
are dead: at dawn in bed the same
white ship spanning the horizon,
and every word the heart denied
sopped up with the daily bread.
The house still waits where shore lights
winked against the bay suggesting,
like old friends, more than they said.

Night again, and time for stars
to stir the shadows on the roof

but no star is in the sky.
Time for a late birdnote or two
to clear the windowpanes
but none comes through as yet.
Still the house keeps beckoning,
bone white and dry inside:

some body should lie down in it.

6

Conrad saw behind the wheel
the unappeasable horizon
where heroes with maddened eyeballs
mounted the ageless waters
on sinful stumps. Who else
could execute, against his heart,
such livid sentences?

The blooded words they whispered
kept thickening into Justice
until the blindfold lifted
and a gunshot blanked them out.

The shot emptied his feelings,
and the ship he manned sails on.

7

To be alive be bold

the boldness branching
from every thing that lives within.
Be hard as stone in silent mire.
Favor the waking
in every speck of being.
Nothing in dirt is dead.
What lies down under the sky
is soon clutched and clutching
to be firm fed
on rock and water.
Kindled in air
it walks the shore
with no need of words.
As Adam wakes and from him Eve
and from them both
the tree risen before them
and before the tree
the willingness to live
that would not die,
the song wells up again

*until the fire-flesh of being
rises to embrace the sky.*

TEETERING

Bark of a tree. Solo. In the rain.

How it is always is.
Changes: outside is seen inside.
Outside changes inside.
Inside looks faster, changing less.
Outside waits till inside goes away.
Outside more slowly always is
only now about to be seen.

In the rain. Solo. Bark of a tree.

POEMS 1976–1980

PROMISE

Let me tell you again
where I must go
back to the farm
without you without them
without you or them

I must go without wife
without sons
and live on the farm alone
feed every animal
draw all the milk myself

I must hear myself breathe
so the song will come
of the wheat I grow
and the power to work
and master the ground

To bury the past in darkness
and wake every day
in the smell of the cold
off the hay and the smart
burn of the wood stove fire

Home will be bearing the tale
of the farm I work
without you without them
while sun smashes down
and rain bears away my life

AFTER THE LETTER

1

*If you happen through again, don't call,
just come by.*
The afternoon you do we speak of the trees'
never-returning
leaves, the power of gradual fulfillment
meaning nothing
in nature but almost everything in our
quick lives,
the body's hard-nosed climb to make it,
and deep down
the consciousness of rot all the while
one pleasures.

We're on our fifth martini, the day
winking through
the leaves, and we swearing never to let
each other go,
when a blue Mercedes slips up the drive
to claim you.
I lunge, surrounding you against its purr.
Your tongue fishes
in my mouth, your rose-lipped body tightening
into mine:
It's so easy to love you! On that lie
I let go.

2

You're drowning in the waves, I'm standing
on a raft
ready for the plunge. Never never will I
rescue you.
Going down, I grapple with a slippery leg,
but already
you've reached bottom, wrapped in a coat
of algae.
My heart sniffs out where you sank,
a boulder
rippling in the sand a century or more.

Still as slime I watch your smile say
*I know you
love me.* I crawl on all fours to feel
around you,
then float over like a dirty handkerchief.
Love, love me!
Quiet as an eye I hear the cry before
the cry began.
To become stone I stop my lungs, I close
my ears,
my pores, my mind. And now to lift you!

LISTEN

Tonight I hear it all spoken,
see it spelled out again
from the window-seat cushion
where the children
you never saw
turned up today
this old V-letter
adorned with your name.

It's the War
speaking through me
writing you,
my apple-cheeked young wife
(dead these six years past):
I'll be home soon again, dear
—my brain half pickled hope,
half jealous fury.

Look how torn up
I manage to be
with words spilling
over the folds
as I sit writing madly
in Paris, in London,
in whory Antwerp,
three, four letters a day,

while hornily plotting
the women I can slip into
and leave curled up behind
until I come on *You darling!*

Faithless evening
hardens round you,
snows your absence
into light.

BEING SOMEBODY

He had need of a way
to be himself
without being himself.

He had so little need
of those who said
they had need of him,

He wanted never to see
any of them again,
though he wouldn't say so.

For once in his life

he was satisfied
simply to be.

To be nobody,
nobody but himself,
himself without himself.

He felt empty and full—
not one or the other
but both at once.

He felt chafed like a child
full of flouting wishes,
floating elations.

But drained of hankerings
like a glass of water
a thirsty man just drank.

He considered someone odd
though familiar may have come
to live inside of him.

Maybe it meant
he was sheltering someone
who needed a home.

He himself had no home,
flitting from friend
to cousin to stranger,

As the occasion demanded,
or urged by the heart,
which he often misread.

He lived everywhere
but at home, where sometimes
he stayed overnight.

Anywhere he slept
he was at home,
if he didn't overstay.

The city he wished most
to live in was nearby
but quite far away.

Near enough to visit
or be visited by
old friends and children,

Far enough off
to forget them all
in a week or a year.

He wanted to live alone
in a den-like apartment,
working nights on his thoughts,

Or in a big rambling house
without tenants and close

to the hub of the city.

He would like also not
to live there but still
to call it his home

Where he could drop in,
surprising himself hard
at work in his study

Or, having been called away,
finding the place
shrieking his absence.

He'd like to live there
and in the country as well,
unknown except for

The gas-meter reader
who'd fade in and
fade out bimonthly.

He once wrote a letter he thought
he'd only half written himself
which ended limply,

"How many empties like me
are there left to pick up
before I die?"

Now he believed the letter
was written completely
by somebody else.

Of course he was wrong—
but what if he was
completely somebody else?

LETTER FROM NEW HAMPSHIRE

now
it would be then
that walking down a snowy road
in the afternoon
under a gray sky
in winter
after it had snowed and would snow
but not yet

when the fir trees by the roadside
with week-old snow clumps
lying iced and heavy
down along the branches
and the twigs of bright green needles
clipped by passing plows

detached and crazy
littering
the too smoothed icy ground

it would be then
just coming into view of
a cottage bouncing up and down
but soon set straight
against the powdered mountain
banked up
on a dense horizon

it would be then
my dear
when thinking started up
to tell me how I missed you
now
that suddenly
the sky ran thin
with speckled afterlight
almost promising
it would not snow today
tonight

it would be then
at first starting of my thinking
of you
that there should negligently
fall into my head
the thought of this grave

heavy handsome
useless world

not needing me
for needing you
for needing me
in boots that leave
their stippled prints in snow
and eyes that take
this crystal quiet in
so quick and slow
and all this
with me or without
should not mean a thing
not anything at all

and when I thought this
then
the sky took back its worried look
grew solid gray
no different than before

except that now
that then
the first few flakes
stirred light
along my sleeve
like afterthoughts of easy living
easy dying
that would later be a heavy fall

it was then my dear
I missed you most
it was then that now
seemed lost the most

it was forever
then

AN ART OF SUMMER

1

Saying a thing is, often makes it—so
the Bible says Jehovah spoke the world.
If I would leap, the mind says,
I would follow! shouts the faithful body.

Word-sperming something into being
works as spirit splitting stone—
or metaphor beclouds till all evaporates.
What time of morning is it? Six o'clock.
And morning's a semaphore of clock hands
locked in a ring of digits.

Entering by chance, the day
becomes you writing in this room as ant

and fly crawl by outside the window squares
against the big leaf-heavy summer trees.

A music you hear accompanying your breathing,
Schubert's last sonata,
sifts through this time placing you on earth
with the fellow-feeling body Schubert knew,
not knowing, writing it at thirty,
he'd die next year, in 1828.

This will-lessness preceding knowing
is what we share receiving
body from body, body into body:
each preformed shape performs its give and take.

Goodbye, Schubert, dead-alive since then,
vale this morning of the crawling ant,
the newly dying birdsong you hear closing
this line—the longest day of 1974.

2

The first leaf shriveling shrivels all belief.

Climbing a giant mossy oak, rose vines
like a passion curling higher
twine belly, arms and spine

till interflowing red and green reverse
the eye as in a dream.

Another tree grows roots like jugular veins
snaking through boulders that impact the trunk.
A sword of lightning smashing the aspen stand
that blocked out sunlight lets in crawling fungi
that chew up most the roots.
One branch escapes, grows new, a crazy crooked
nearly leafless arm upthrust in sunlight, the rest
choking in a tangle of devoured wood.

Torn-off leaves that cry *adorn adorn*
are still unconscious of their separateness.
Adornment is the form severed things take on
in their bewilderment—
the doom awaiting those that lie apart.

Parting the meadows, gardens gone astray—
the red and palpitating coquelicots,
claws of yellow honeysuckle, pistils
shivering, the wolfly lycopods and couch grass,
sweet mignonettes, the green and gray plebians,
stonecrop fleshy, corymbs of pungent yarrow,
wild chervil's umbellets,
rose-colored commack and the milk-white crosswort—
grow dreaming someone calls them each by name.

The first leaf shriveling shrivels all belief.

3

Waking next day you walk, half sleeping, out,
as cawings, squeaks and casual chirps turn off,
to see through glued-up flowers an eagle,
landed from nowhere, at the crossroad facing you,
gigantic as the truth of feeling, a cause
more than a feeling, an eagle so big
it must portend something startling.

You stand with the day curved around you
and only the eagle to answer the questions
what brought him? what keeps him?
inferred by his ambling toward you, then off,
as though giving you time to escape.

Was it laid out for eagle and man to meet?
Was it intended because one was human
one might go on doing this and that,
meet so and so, go around there again
only to miss meeting such and such,
maybe cave in to end in a place
where only one could now end up?

With your first head-turn he ruffles his feathers
from talons to beak, and trundling out
to a wider clearing takes off
in a slow air-banging cyclone,
leaving you pinned to the tip of his vortex,
his rising surrounding the sky.

Was it a sleep or was it to end in a sleep—
so someone, no doubt related, might now awaken
to see enough, not wanting or actually knowing
enough, to pick up the thread?

Was the eagle at last a sign of it all
or witness—summoned or summoner?
And now as he floats, a speck in the eye of the sky,
are there words to waken the sleeping dreamer asking
and answering himself in the eagle?

> *—Eagle, what is it you do
> descending to the norm
> then climbing beyond my eyes?*
>
> *—In the mothering of matter
> learning to survive
> the fathering of form.*

STARTING THE HOSTILITIES

We've cleared the wires where
the hostages hung all night.
Feeling is up,
horses kick at the barn doors,

youngsters in town
round up the old pistols,
some test improvised bombs,
wives quietly clean rifles.

This is no child's tourney,
there'll be other casualties.
The veterans are growling
We'll tear our their hearts . . .

PASSIONFLOWER

We grew the miraculous flower:
five corpse-white spokes
sunk in pubic hair
with that radial penumbra
just hovering over
the flimsy purple core—
and sat there gloating, ah,
the triumph after such care!

How long did it last?
till a painter sat down
and put it all into a sketch
before it could wilt from view.
Then from his painting

came so many feasts
for we can't count
how many eyes.

But no trace at all
of our passionate growth.
A bush of dark mint,
too vigorous, bunches up there,
assailing the air,
and now in that corner
where two fences met
flaps the painter's folding chair.

OPENING

   gray lips

   this hour's
   hourless light
   turns
   not yet rising

   opening
   gray lips

   morning
   labors

wet mouthed
on pig iron gates

a woman
who cannot
rise
there lies

impaled

I NEED YOU

What the two windows want:
   the bridge and the cycle
and the tree cut down.

What the whitewash wants:
   the cold milky ground,
the tombstone missing a name.

What the cracked roof wants:
   the lovers in bed long dead
unmaking the child

already grown to a man
   groping past loving, past light,
roped to the end of his life.

AFTER THE SEPARATION

Back to your room
after my weekend visit,
you play underseas war
using the closet & windowseat bay
for submarine lairs,
your mouth devising
flesh & gun disintegrations
coughing fast-flashing sallies up
out of mind

I see your dark pupils
figure the damage—
Is it worth shoveling up
just to get on with now?

There's a blind man under the bed
wanting to show you where to hide
when the homework stacked
like tank-flattened GIs
gets punishingly high.

"Daddy, I'm frightened—
or maybe just bored,"
you want to cry
as my car miles off
turns screeching back.

I pound & pound
on the big front door.

THE HOUSE

The house killed by your word
withstood much deeper wounds
before it let go.
Those were years we lived
wrangling inside
without daring to ask
should we patch it or part.

Those absentee summers
neighbors by moonlight
were statues
climbing the trees,
training their mirrors of air
at the windows,
were we dead or merely asleep?

Night snowfalls in winter
imprisoned bulls
charged beeches and pines
hunched in the driveway
till eased off
by ploughs next morning,
the bright air a diamond.

Those were years the lawn
thickened and spread,
having no care
as the weathers ran wild,
small vandal gangs

assaulting and dying,
child by child.

Dogging all-night refusals
day-calms and word-gusts
pretended relief.
At breakfast some mornings
we sat like vacationers
facing the bay
already polluted.

Now a goldfisted flagpole
thrust from the lawn
against vengeance
and vandals
that crept up regardless
stands flagless,
detached from the house.

Last summer new lights
riddled the waters,
night planes hurtling
through air
cleared the heat of neighbors
still churring
and scorching the grasses.

Exclude, exclude, echoes the house.
Dead rattan rockers nod
in a desert of sunlight

as we leave, separate,
and the new owner's eyes
smilingly rise
from the lawn.

MONSTER TALK

The sight of me finished and lost
till another one comes but not yet
and who knows how soon

The sight of me gone and done for
over the fence and nothing
but tracks in the woods

The sight of me never again
to crack open an eye and murder
your sleep at two a. m.

The sight of me landing all over
with kisses I gave you holes
in the belly and thighs

The sight of me lurking at table
drymouthed with it without it
in sunlight in fog

The sight of me slipping away
sliding off all the mirrors
down all the drains

You can wake now without me
the nightmare of me is over
try breathing again

and dream up the day when
the big advertised monster
out of your mind

gropes at the windows and doors
to crawl over you the shadow
wished home tonight

DIALOGUE IN THE SLEEPING HOUSE

The lacquered brown wall reddens

> *like our own wishes*
> *we are carved out of air*

touched by the afternoon sun

> *the part of us feeding a wish empowers*
> *then lives past it*

warming and worming its way

> *while the wish exists it lives*
> *apart from the empowering part*

deep through the windows

> *because to exist a wish needs*
> *detachment from what feeds it*

as if to engrave its light

> *the possibility to continue detached*
> *is probably almost infinite*

in the sleeping house forever

WITHOUT LOVE

Without love
the gift grows real—
a pebble slipped
from an unclenched palm
dazzles the broken ground.

PASSES FOR NICANOR PARRA

Think of an old friend who died
Now turn in your chair and he's there
filling the doorway smiling

Rise and he walks straight towards you
Leave the room and he sits in your chair
waiting for you to enter smiling

*

Almost at ease with your wife and children
you sail out to an island together
At the helm you know the boat is sinking

You tell them   They try bailing out   Too late
You leap overboard   Gasping you turn
The boat sails by and they are cheering

*

Evidence piles up day by day
we do not live
where we are living

We refurbish   Add a wing
Rearrange the bed   And
houses eat us as we sleep

*

Who sits so close when you try to rise

If only he'd move or stand up by himself
you'd spring to your feet in a flash

You make a last effort but it's no use
You turn at him to glare
He is weeping inconsolably

PARTITA

Somewhere I am,
low-lying,
I cannot come to rest—
on the mountain
the river
underneath me
almost sleeping.

Somewhere I was,
tide rising,
I heard a gliding
up the beach
of heavy wings
near me and I
just waking.

Somewhere I'll be,
riding home,

lights let me
round an old darkness
to the children
sleeping in the house
my coming rouses.

THE PAINTER IN THE MOUNTAIN
(for Lorna)

"Can I love if I have such pain inside?
The piano playing in the mountain
tells me where I am,
filling sound with color.

This summer afternoon could be
an open desert where two lovers meet:
Melissa leans into the grand piano
making music, making love.
Arthur singing what he wants her playing
stands behind; listening,
she drops her fingers.

Outside trees pour sunlight
and the mountain hurls it back again.
In the air trying to fill a space,
my hard pain asks the mountain:
love my paper, touch my brushes,

press color into them,
until my painting fills what is
no longer missing."

FOR HIS MOTHER FLYING INTO HER SEVENTY-SEVENTH

If there were ploughs in heaven
you'd break ground with one—
not for casting seed
but to open new earth there
as if to say See, it can
be done and done by me alone.

If there were a place to burn
in deeper suffering you'd ride
a razor wind there, outsped
only by special grace
of your falling body's thinking it
the first to feed that fire.

May pardon come for your forever
nursing a grousing mother
into her final silence
there in that house
so you alone might come alive
to make her bed and lie in it.

STUMBLING OUT OF THE PRADO

>time lives
>through eyes
>and faces
>bulging to see
>who we are
>
>the sweet music
>hardening
>parades of victims
>stammering
>storm troopers
>
>and Goya
>deaf to questions
>burning in his own
>man-eaten
>freedom

RILKE'S WHITE HORSE

>I remember a day in spring, at evening, in Russia.
>
>A white horse, his hobbled fetlock wrenching his stride,
>gallops down the village lane, his black mane

whipping his neck until he bursts into the empty
moonlit meadow, rearing to a standstill.

The night he whinnies at a moment is ponderously still,
heedless of his blood beating a music that becomes,
louder than his heavy breathing, his whole being,
his heart waiting to be heard and understood.

Now may this fable be his song forever.

ANOTHER MARCH

    Climbing the scrawny women,
    the plastic virgins,
    I came on a field
    laid out for planting,
    bones in piles
    along the wire fences
    and a spindly scarecrow
    overlooking it.

    In the salt marsh
    a mile away
    the neighbor's chimney
    was barely smoking,

and the sky
overcast as usual
hinted of the bitter cold
that was on its way.

The field glittered
in remembered sunlight.
A wind knifed through me,
turning the scarecrow
this way and that.
As I began to dance
the women hunched behind me
laughed and laughed.

COME

Beyond her in the red house
glow the crystal flowers,
the green lake furled for winter,
and the idea
of fruitfulness next year.

For she is aware of the seed
who runs the furrowed earth,
and in her head

are all the generations
waiting in the ground.

'In her the seed will bear
the whole of summer
next and after next,
already giving off the flavor
of ripening and decay.

Now all around her waits
the grave red house
with knives and dishes set,
till at the door
the fainting fathers come.

NIGHT ISLAND

The boat lights pass, the window smarts,
wakening to the night the dim island
floating like a string of whales,
the sky a sunken eye the sea devours.

It comes to this: the leached-out world
has masked the hidden boulders
like an oyster in a broken shell.
What cries for light in the sucking shore?

SWEEPING THE ROOM

We give birth to ourselves
on the brink of dying.
Others stand there
sorrowing, pitying,
not yet born,
shudder and ogle
this negligible dying.

How do we tell them
they too will burst with
last eyesight breaking,
sweeping the room
of the husks of children
not knowing who dies
is coming alive
to them yet unborn?

LAST SONG

You are asleep at my center,
a recently emptied volcano,
with ashes still sifting through air,
and I, remembering the old heat
in it, remember you as I

almost land without touching
the innocent hills and valleys,
till nowhere becomes a drifting,
a new withdrawing and build-up
of all my wasted forces.

G. W. M.

My neighbor is dead.
His hands are held by a weight
no longer his own.

They have shut down his stare
and we steer
through the close of his eyes.

Don't say his death
is your death is my death.
He died alone.

We who have lived as he lived
this dog of a life
part on that note.

Now each to his bone.

PABLO NERUDA

Under reason and steel grows the final poem of your death
in the city where you were the house of your breath,
smoked out, ransacked, squandered in shreds,
as under the stones precise on the heights
you guessed they had buried the rags of slaves.

As under the seal of wax there clacked
in the general's beak the white-tongued admiral,
giving the acid word of steel in the guts
to your guarded brightness, life, with its shadow
invisibly wearing away the heaviest stone.

In your light blatant or hidden forever
under the everyday sky exposed
like a maundering madman mocked into meaning—
because no one can bear the darkness alone,
because no one can go on shielded alone,

Your name went up in the half light that day,
like smoke lolling up from the cannon's mouth,
from house after house and cell after cell,
to show where the flowering multiple death
had departed your body, your country, its ghettos.

As your life's first day is destroyed in the last,
as the mouth of the serpent swallows its tail,

as the spirit's skyscraper's consumed in a rose,
let all darkness be broken like bread among brothers,
all being more and less than a metaphor.

THREE MOMENTS FOR GEORGE SULLIVAN

1 *Burial in Providence*

Your sleeping eye
turned inward now
in death
is looking squarely
at me

I have none to know you
and only yours
to see me
wanting for my own
to follow

Do not wait long
for earth to come
settling in with you
for the loose stones
to shift towards you

Help me remind
the heavy quiet
you have come to lie in
with the mother
that bore you

to the new sleep
stretched straight
with no need
nuzzling you to be
growing over earth

or in the sea floating
or turning in air
to the cities
of the mind's
altering necessities

Give me with you
sinking slowly under
my feet turning
this next moment
in your vanishing eye

2 *Waiting in Washington*

In the bruised sky
racing
my scanning eye
and the withered tree
measuring
a low fury of wind
I catch trills
whistling
the ends of days

A time that was
will come
in the couplings
of underground fur
feeding asleep
root and worm
beast and mind
to meet overground

In the warm hide's
last days and hours
still smoking with breath
the panes of the eyes
snow mountains
stone slides
clear to the end

Time moves down forests
past toy cities fallen
through heads cracked
with flashings
whisked into brains
like mine

Last week died
with my friend
tucked in his box
and my stare
gave him pause
a wet second on earth
in the sky's face
in the wind's eye closing

In the airport
I sit under rain
waiting to fly

3 *Walking in Sweet Briar*

On the path
the thawing rivulets
of icebound mud
run an ooze my shoes
cannot resist

I plod upward
towards the first
lit window of a house
soon to pass
in twilight

when from nowhere
comes a shattering
as of all things
fallen in
their emptiness

a breaking
of the clots
and clogs of days
as I arch
through rain

too slight
to threaten
reminding how once
in skyfuls
it cracked down

and I ran
as though all life
were funneling
off beneath
my shoes

Lives tunnel
in their safeties
making room
beyond me
as I move unheard

back into my life
of nowhere's
other silence
other time
awaiting

the first word to be
before words
were heard
singing the way
this ooze runs

under me
before me
moving past the house
it will take
after me

THE AFFINITIES OF ORPHEUS

THROUGH YOU

Glass I've wanted to live
through you
to be returned to me so

I'd drink the light I see
where you live
in a time you'll always be

without knowing I am
watching me
appear there in you when

wishing not to be ends
with your silent
Now walk through me

HIS DREAM

How he had sat
huddled all night
failed faces passing
the narrowing light
the windswept street
watching the fire
die in its ashes

How from the ashes
he learned of root forces
the powerful hand
that would crack
the light open
the day he must break
to be born

HIS CHAIN

How he had made
link after link
thinking loosely to join
not to imprison
each to its self
and worlds apart
then when it jarred
he suddenly turned

ANOTHER

within this leaf
a life
within this life
a soul

with messages
trees hear
inhere
as we who are
cohere
in what we see

while
toward
this tree
this leaf
we
only
may appear
to be
and bear
apart

A WIND DIES

A wind lies down
Nothing in the tree
but frozen space
between the leaves

No sound
but underneath
the tree a shadow

strains to feel
the tree is moving
wind in the leaves
still passing

A wind has died forever
A tree forever frozen
deepening a shadow
tears itself to pieces

MELTING SONG

Fire be Water

Hear Fire reply

I am Water already
all things you dream of you see
rainfall the tree
perfect limbs drowning
me they become that am you
drifting a breath
burning to Earth

Cried the Earth
cried the Air

Water be Fire

And Water
silently nodded
I am

ANOTHER ORPHEUS

Hear him waken
parades
bell toll
fire gong

the sea
never failing
exploding earth
carnival

Leave him naked
dazzling
in a room
alone

A first holiday
barely turning
he becomes all
one mirror knows

His last day
a rope

slaps the rafter
laughter below

doors tearing open
a crashing upstairs
love him you
he will never know

JOY: AN END SONG

I heard joy speak to me
your joy and the time spent
neither wishing nor having it
before it came
after it went

I tasted it through you
your joy and the spending of it
the time it was
the being of it
your presence in it

What was possible
and what became of it
the loss already known
just as it came
just as it went

Knowing your joy
was neither having it
nor having you
but what lay open once
between the two

Between the diver
and his breath
the waiting shadow
and the body
lying down in it

LINES FOR DANCERS

Dolls remember
waiting to be born

an empty turmoil
in the head

the memory
of milk

a quiet shifting
in the straw

*

The body straight
the body folded
then poise
altering the center
the difficult
destruction
of a thoughtless
balance

      *

The sexual body
dropping
in a chair
in bed
under him
on her

down

and the neutral
wisdom
to rise
again
from broken
stances

up

      *

Gesture after gesture
sometimes hardens them

the music stops
but nothing can slacken them

curled up on their sides
night and day

bodies dance to reproduce themselves
with all their might

and faces lock
desperate to be blank

WHO

It is your last day and hour and you are alone
You have nothing to say even to yourself
Your mind is almost blank
A fly is buzzing in the room
You can kill the fly but you don't   Your
thoughts will not move you   Without color or
depth they skim across your mind   Before you
can read them they disappear

Now after ten minutes or thirty you begin to hear the sound of words spoken words

You think   Who speaks   You are greedy for another sound another presence

Who speaks   Who is speaking

It is a half-friendly   Who   Like your mother when you were a child   Soft round voice with the querulous edge

The words fade   The voice goes over the edge and disappears

You look around the room   It is bare but things are in it your mind will not name

You look around the room twisting your neck turning your shoulder

You stoop you kneel you lie down

You get up quickly

The voice with the words opens up again

Who you ask

Be still

Who

Be still be still

A silence grows breaking into the voice slowly speaking as you listen word quickening faster more lively

Who

You think   It is like my father

No

You think   It is like him

Him

Him the other one

  No
  You think   It is like myself in him
  Yes
    It is coming faster   turning the
room   turning you on your knees again   The
ceiling moves down
    Words pour out faster clearer fresher full of
feeling never before spoken   words never
heard before out of you
    You they say You they say You they say You
    You YouYou   YouYouYouYou   Breaking
loose they surge out of your chest   you
pushing to join them till you are all at once all
of them in a long water flowing widening
flooding an ocean sea world all water without
earth or sky a water all over water gone over
forever

FOUR SPRINGS

SPRING ONE

Suffused by paint-cracking warmth in a steam-heated room,
late winter rain
slushing away through the snow, the traffic, the auto horns
bleating and shaking
their cages outside, I linger behind pulled shades
lost in the dumps
of my own stock presence; with armies caught stark on the edge
of command slowly tearing
their minds awake, I loll half-dozing, attuned to
the rise of a day
embalming the mouth, muting the whistle of play,
the *twitch twitch* of birds
in the melting boughs of a grimy New England day;
gripped in the bowels
of a gray tabernacular house, I lie photographing
the self—myself,
all selves, bright and to fade, as once Mathew Brady,
in innocent camps
of suffering, snapped the tired grim lounging dying
Blue and Gray.

. . .

The President stands up to hundreds of millions, a dog
among dogs barking
into the bags of their heads (". . . honor in war . . ."),
lapping their brains;
they listen, they roll on their backs, huffing, surprised,
feel something slip

(". . . our boys are dying for us . . ."), believing only
something has failed,
like a bad job for too long, or the man who has kept it, vanished,
leaving behind
his family but no other trace, like a dime
dropped in a sewer,
yet this man is also the nation, thrashing, distending
itself until,
no longer a man, it subsides in the dark and becomes
the thing that is gone.

. . .

I find a man sitting inside myself and leering pedantically.
I let him. I take on his smirk and voice, pitched low.
It relieves me
to be him—small, ceremonious, hedgy, a stuffy
nonentity.
It is always someone quite distinct, somebody
I can name:
an insolent clerk, ogre lady or punitive person
long forgotten.
Where do they suddenly come from? What dredges them up?
I borrow them
like a dirty old jacket I like to wear because
it's so worn,
so ugly, ill-fitting, and because it becomes me.
As a child I was told,
Don't frown—the look will stick to your face forever.
Look mom, I'm frowning.
Look dad, someone I'm not has really become me.
I'm Lon Chaney,

the hunchback of Notre Dame, the Jekyll devouring
odd Mr. Hyde!
The only nice thing about them is that they're disguises
I can easily drop,
like a secret pride, an attitude I must try out,
then quickly discard
when it gets in the way of—what? my being myself?
That's piously said,
but what is it? The truth is it rankles, this having
to take on somebody
else's old smell, ego-fatuous speech and smile.
It punishes me.
They've gotten the upper hand and I'm fighting them all—
punitive ogre,
insolent pedant, weird little bogies, swarming through
the unkillable dark.

. . .

Brute, wise man, ogre, and beauty, cripple and President;
infant, dwarf,
and pygmy; dotard, darling, enemy, friend,
intellectual giant;
ancient Egyptian, Lestrigonian, Socrates, Moses,
Marx and Hitler;
the wife you sleep with, the mother and father you no
longer live with;
the son you know from the cradle, the fool and the bore
you know at a glance;
all wear inside them—who can tell why or how?—
an all-covering "I,"
an all-weather voluminous self that begins with the fetus's
first flimsy heartbeat

and stretches on out to the last inaudible fall
of the pulsing brain—
everyone that has ever lived, since mankind began,
has worn inside him,
indelibly fixed, an unchangeable picture of exactly
the person he is,
like the silhouette ivory cameo piece grandma wore,
having inside it
the prize tinted portrait of her as she was at sixteen—
and which, whether looked at
or not, each of us, secretly bearing, regards
as the "real me."

. . .

As spring comes back each year with its new work and cares—
a breaking of hardness
never repaired or repairable, season of ooze,
of uneasy lures,
into wild air where streetcries and birdcalls ascend
like darting balloons;
into the lilting of summer robing, disrobing, which
people past thirty
no longer feel as a call in the blood (Do people
past thirty plan
all the wars?), the peeling of skins, mutation of genes,
degeneration
of bones, in the garden weeds rampantly growing, shooting up
even through asphalt—
comes the asking, Who will survive into summer with nothing
itself but the self
palely regarding the natural unselfregarding
fornications of objects

and bodies . . . cries in the air . . . artilleries . . . gouging
of wounds . . . rich blood
caking where dead men no longer lie . . . cattle
peacefully drinking
at home, in Vietnam . . . and, in Teotihuacán,
drawn on a pillar,
". . . a jaguar singing . . . under his mouth, water; . . . a priest wearing
the robes of a god."

. . .

High noon. It's time to get up—jump into my pants,
run out and dance
in the foggy streets of Providence, play God—
maybe bring out the sun!

SPRING TWO

The days are gentler, frosts are paper thin.
In these parts
winter is hard. You spend it bracing, then succumbing
to floating fevers
prone with your own ghost in bed, wrapped around
your viruses
like a wet mat, hating your flesh, all flesh.
Outside, the winners
go eating up the track while you drift off
with a temperature
of one hundred and three, thrown by empty self-
effacing dreams.

. . .

In one I see a man sitting way beyond me
at the other end
of the room, smoking or pretending to smoke, in a wing-
backed easy chair,
with the back facing me, and not seeming to care
if he's seen.
The room is dim and I'm straining to see what he's at.
He's very busy,
but the harder I look, the darker the room becomes.
His pace increases:
he's grim, working quickly, ferociously stuffing an oversized
man-shaped coat
with blankets, filling it out, all black, and making it
into a figure
that if casually looked at would seem like a person sitting
there backwards, smoking,
in a wingbacked chair. It dawns on me then that what
he's straining to do
is make an escape without being noticed, even
while being observed:
getting away while giving the appearance (the dummy
he's stuffed) of being
still there. And now he comes moving on all fours,
but too swiftly; just passing
under a nearby table, smoking, the cigarette
stuck to his lips,
the red coal of it burning, and he coming on
shaggy and fast,
an inflated roach, ever nearer (my God!) to me, and aiming
to go—where? Through me!

. . .

How was it in childhood almost to have died?
It was to live,
beyond the sickness and the being small,
having touched
the mushy border splashing, plowing through
the hot black aching
sickroom ten days of night unending, then surfacing
(like the picture book seal
coughing itself up on a beach) in blinding daylight
to eat and drink
among the bumbling shapes of life: on the still
sad side table
the torn tan lampshade, leftover breadcrumbs, bedpan,
cloth and soap,
watching the nurse's curd-white fingers pause,
the one with a gold
wedding band (saying *I belong to someone*),
bracing the fever
chart, and sunlight jerking down the wall.

. . .

It was to live,
though still a child and parented, beliefless
as a man
and parentless: divorced parents, what have I
to do with thee?
It was to live pretending what one's parents gave
or wished to give
was still the true umbilicus and only
necessary lifeline,
but absolutely immaterial. Fawned on,
to smile back.

Having wandered by the swamp all day, to come home
late, contrite,
to shouts of castigation, whispering *I'm sorry*,
but not to mean it.
It was being still a child but no longer someone's,
belonging to no one
inside one's own great empty endless self.

. . .

It was lifelong to be his only brother's death,
as in the poem which read:

> *sometimes I hear the taste and smell of me*
> *crack like a bag of spontaneous rags*
> *under warm snow*
>
> *sound like smell strong enough*
> *I can taste it—*
> *it has to be me*
> *that still might be*
> *any child you know must die*
> *who will survive in you—*
>
> *who knows?—died*
> *survived*
>
> *a small brother died*
> *mack trucked in the May warm*
> *macadam Brooklyn street*
> *just as the sun winked me past him*
> *just as my shadow slipped me on*
> *to the iron front house door*

*a schoolboy hung on a handle
hearing one pierced cry
the driver's glowering curse*

*afraid if I turned I would see
still in the trickle
spread wet and red
the soon caking blood
caught in the blond hair
stuck to the tread
picked up
head swooped back over
the driver's elbow*

*whisked white necked
into a sudden cab
siren fading in smoke*

*left
forever to whisper
let it be me
so I could hear whispering back
not yet
not me*

*left
all day watching all night
till early
that morning
the nurse floated down
a clean white pigeon*

*wiping her mouth saying he
the boy is dead*

it can't be

he
maybe it's me

and I can't tell
sunk in a bag
and can't breathe

. . .

Coming back from New York on the New Haven Line, the day
hovered raw and gray,
oozing in through the window. I floated out with it,
into it, watching,
observed, all the way back to Providence.
Then the poem
that came through seemed written *through* me as through glass:

Spring Northbound

Leafmold prepares the ground.
    A hidden star wakes.
        An unknown star discovers night,
    moonlight on snow in crevices.
Piles of ermine break the ground.

A lemon haze flares up
    among stripped trees,
        naming a source there.
    Sight returns and twitters.
Light stands among the trees.

Litters of seen things
 unknown to one another
  meet touching, still,
 but in the scratchy light
no thing moves.

The winter worm is still.
 Ice glaze shrivels
  on the pond twitching
  like a wrong skin
 going to be shed.

Stripes of frost-white
 ooze the ground,
  threading, tunnelling,
  undercutting
ground from ground.

Whiteness vanishes in sound,
 pebbles going down,
  potsherds, snail shells,
 flakes of tin—
ghosts of themselves.

Detritus of things once known
 making a language
  that suddenly at 30, 40, 50,
 with enough death inside,
one day you hear trickling,

spreading quietly, breaking
 into many waters.
  O waters of Babylon,
  how they sing,
 how they weep,

telling how that ancient
   sound of leaving
     after words long ended,
   gone out of time and hearing,
begins to form again,

as words worrying stones,
   clicking among dead shapes,
     convoking with others
   against what passes,
wanting to be known,

tell this (this! only this!):
   Drag off the dead
     rooted in the dead.
   Uncover the live waters
of the singing god,

hissing in yet-to-open mouths,
   dumbly shaping sound
     of flesh and horn
   from this breaking
ooze and flow.

Down whispering sheen
   on wet bark quizzing light
     (Where, where have you been?)
   trees stretch into
a spryness flying,

over stonecrop coming,
   by rockwalls massing
     in a bulb-brown breaking up
   of clumps below
where the fox's footprint fades.

So may I, as this northward train
rips by the earthborne changes,
once for all be measuring
the dying in me needed
to begin the being born.

SPRING THREE

A woman plays life
like a waterfall outpouring all-in-one,
an endlessness
we feel in music as it is shaped by our hands,
mouths and lungs
agrapple, impounding the all-abundance of being—
all but the source,
then stopping, once emptied of joy, on coming to be,
as in death's calmness
dissolving, resuming the flesh, to cry out of darkness,
beginning to breathe.

If fire's the source, it's there that being arises
in shapeless air,
as in the dreaming of mothers endowing, instilling
their offspring-to-be,
from first heartbeat to the pounding shriek of being
born, unearthed.
When it is, it breathes—the rest is aftermath.
Mated or mismated,
she insists to the end that her honor's a mixture of passion,
possessed and possessing,
towards the creation that hangs on the words *I do*,
their vow to the earth,
the deed which only awaits the spread of the seed.

Trial and error,
more trial against error, since incubation in her
is the ageless wild flood
of the cells' multiplication in search of the singular
simple conformance
that will shape the child against intricate odds or fail.
In her getting
is her begetting, in the pleasuring lock-bodied lust
the mindless matrix
starting up her mindfulness—and from this there follow
all law, all beauty,
all cancer, and beautiful cancered society:
from caves and earthworks,
our borders and walls, our house, roof, and furniture,
excluding all others,
to protect the future rocked in the past, put a face
on the human nest.

SPRING FOUR

The interminable colors of life flow through me with this
light rain, each downward
stroke a feeling or thought looking slantingly strange,
neither mine nor not mine,
belonging to anyone living or maybe not: maybe
only to those
dead and dying that chance to flash through to me here just now
while I take things in,
soaking up, thoughtless, everything happening now,
all that's passing
and coming to be, while the rain goes battering down
the grasses and leaves,

wetting houses and animal faces, slowly changing the faces
of bombarded children
in far jungle villages, pinned down under huts
that fold into flames,
surprised to be drenched as they lie there dying and staring
up in the rain

By this drenched old house over the Tagus from Lisbon,
an elephant-eared
banana tree is clattering—the rain having sharpened
almost to hail,
the last fruit eaten, the new in its viscous buds
beginning to stir.
A gold bantam rooster has just started over the checkerboard
cobblestone sluices
that take on infinite shadings of God knows what
reflections of light
thrown off by a tense pine forest looking spacious as death
back of the wall.
And these shadings of light before me fall as though brushed
through crisscrossing webs
to glint in the swift and vigorous rain, impending
for days and insisting
the way one insists when thinking he'll last forever.

. . .

The papers say six chairs around a table
are changing the world.
Whose men are in the chairs? And whose ideas
are in their heads?
They do not look at one another—they look
at nothing; they hear,
they speak, they think of nothing. They are dead.

. . .

The world is changing as we think it. Thinking
is a flame burning.
Thinking is in the head where nothing happens.
Thinking happens
inside the flame. The flame will go on burning,
The flame is nothing.

Thinking is like tomorrow. Tomorrow will
have windows. It will
have windows out of which we look, and we look
through windows which
reflect our eyes. In our eyes there are windows,
not made of glass,
not made of windows. Our eyes are the windows
our thoughts burn.

. . .

Tomorrow will happen. The flame will burn. Nothingness
will appear.

. . .

I follow my words like an ant on his pile among piles,
and they sing to me—
the music my words make when I read them in print. I smile,
I purr, my eyes'
Pygmalion rubs lover hands over them, and all because . . .
no, not just because . . .

I made them—they're no longer me, I love them only
momentarily.
The music passes, its loveliness turns sour—
a dying fall,
enough, no more. Is this because it is

no longer me
but spoken memory congealed in *Was* and, like
the child I was,
looks like me and likes me? Rather, looks
like what I dreamt
I wished that I could be, if words put down,
just so, could make
so firm a thing as Me or Mine, something
I'd never be—
never be but not know it . . . yes, and know it
but still not know it:
in words converting me I'd find what I dreamed
I had to be.
And who'd think of dreaming this dream of me but a Me
lots better than me?

. . .

My heart is a love that I like and dislike a bit more,
a bit less, than a friend.
It turns like a world half-known that is huge and cold
as the moon still-a-moon,
And you don't remember me, it says, *because*
I've always been there.
You bear with me as you would with a parent you care for
more the less
that you see, the longer you live to remember as younger
than you are now.

Oh world, my heart, as you live and sleep, remember me
less and less,
but bear with me to wake to the stars and the moons
always there to land on
in dreams when the earth, grand mother-father of life,
is no longer there.

SPRING JOURNAL: POEMS

THE DEAD

You want to bring them back.
Would they, if they could, return,
after such a heavy crossing?
You try, until the wish, almost
disattached, gnawing, growling,
finally bursts loose to call them.

You look up, and they are there:
alert, much younger, fresher, dancing
in the special fragrance
that becomes them, absorbed
in nothing else but this,
this lilt of theirs, their fullest being!

You rush toward them joyfully
when the cry cuts you (is it
out of you or them or whom?),
and you are nowhere, caught and straining
to the faintest, farthest echo
fading,
     "Edwin! Edwin!"

HER HAND

She was sleeping an animal sleep
I couldn't make out.

When she woke, the animal sucked,
thinning her face, drowning her mouth.
She drooled and her hand
went at the flecks, vaguely,
purpling the neckskin,
splotched, worn out.
The hand tightening up
went dead on the coverlet.

Dead, but it spoke. It said,
"You will die, you must die."
And I spoke to the hand alone.
"Move," I said. And it moved.
It scurried a bit in the bed,
living a life of its own.
It moved, moving her, not her eyes.
It was hers and not hers.
It was dead, but ordered
by me, it quivered alive.

It didn't want me, it didn't want her.
It had to be what it was without us.
She may not have known it—
squaring herself, almost raising
her shoulders alive,
but the hand, forcing her down,
told her in sleep she would die.
I still follow the end of her sleep:
her animal wide mouth wiped out,
her hand a cinder in the ground.

FOR MARGOT

Almost fallen asleep
in the song of your face,
I tell myself vaguely
to waken and snatch it
at once, so close to
my hearing, or lose it
forever, be lost.

This music that passes
before words begin
streams through your face,
from the interlocked print
of centipede lashes
to the thinning gold down
ambushing your mouth,

and composes a song
my eyes close to keep
from breathing away.
Should I waken or not?
Enraged by the doubt
I hover, now nearing,
now backing away,

until—what's this?
Your smile wakens eyes,
skies open wide!
Dazzled, still leaning

to hear, my head
drops into its own
Icarus pratfall,

dizzying down
to cacophonous kisses,
in rapids of your
tongue-glistening mouth,
drowning my "Am I . . .
and is this . . . and what was . . .
the song of your face?"

BIRTH SONG: IN THE WING SEAT, AT NIGHT
(for Daniel, born 1966)

1

See the pink light,
tiny and blinking,
now on, now off,
on a plane wallowing,
a light
swallowed by darkness,
swallowing darkness.

This is my immersion—
I, a traveller,
someone carried,
carrying his blood,
in darkness,
on a plane between lights,
between night and day
(a deathday, a birthday),
travel cross-country,
wrapped in still air,
knowing only
(through living a dying)
the end will be landing.

2

Wait!

The end is so near,
it is beginning,
we are beginning.
A light is blinking,
pink as a doll.

A child is beginning,
nearing zero.
A starlight approaches.

I am he,
the one thinking,
the traveller.

And the child to be born
(*already born,*
you will say,
it has happened before),
now waiting
at the end of the journey
is almost here by me.

About me, people, like me,
travelling unknowing
(many men, many women),
waiting to die,
to be born.

The pink light
still blinking up on the wing,
doll-like, in sight,
and starlight approaching,
a child being born.

3

How shall I know who he is,
now so clearly beside me,
I who am living
knowing I'm dying?

Son! Brother! Creature! Being!
Man dying is
being born!

Over the blinking in darkness
a light, an aura
of fondness is widening.

Soon, my love, soon
as the starlight
approaches and brightens,
let this plane down.

4

Land hurtles to meet us,
bathed wholly
in blood light.

We land in a clatter of darkness.
The blinking is gone.

Son, brother, child,
alight with me now.
We are carried no more.

See, we have passed over,
newborn.

SECOND SON DAY
(for Margot, mother of us)

On this fleshy pink, too sunny afternoon
I note the riotous control of flowerbeds
in the civil, dogbarking air of Berkeley.

All one's innerness draped everywhere
in punishing detail, externalizing memory
in a climate too favorable for nostalgia.

I close my eyelids from the glare and think
only what I want to think—nothing
unpleasant, nothing too spectacular.

I am forty-seven and the just-made father
of a second son, downy Jeremy, asleep in the portico.
I doze to older Daniel spitting in a rage.

And dream I am the older son who gangs up
on his minute brother, slapping him awake:
"How could you intrude on us, we happy three?

You'll never be the darling I am to them.
I'll see to that. I'll nail you to a tree!"
My eyes jerk open, head pounded by a sneeze.

(A tent of gossamer, striped rainbow or pale bass,
invades the lemon tree, teems down on periwinkle.
Are they bands of feeding butterflies or bees?

Then something like a donkey's half-eaten head,
sunken at the feet of peonies, gets swamped by them,
trickling light like honey from a trough.

Do eyes deceive, focused only on the stuff
one wishes to believe? Well, what of it!
Eyes are the fine beginnings of ideas.

Ideas that may not please. So praise the bees,
if that is what they are, and light, if that's it.
I have mine and they have theirs to feed.)

Bless me, Margot, Daniel, just-born Jeremy!

NATIVITY

Toward the child came starlight,
the light of his world and mine,
the light of the world he'd yet
to perceive and divine.

Birds, fishes, and men
drew breath with the child,

as if born again,
the dead moving toward starlight.

"Man is King of this life,"
sang the starlight.
"The hunger for death must die.
Man is divine."

Now birds, fishes, and I
hear our blood sing reply
in the newborn child,
opening the eyes of the child.

RACE

I look at you and tremble, smiling.
What are you thinking?
Am I the king your husband?
Some dead fish? Anyone at all?
Do I know you? Say I do.
Do I content you? Often, mostly.
Do you contain me? If not you,
who else would, could or should?

The day jams up with clouds,
far white sails striving

in the bay that sweeps them
out to the dark-mouthed sea.
Coolly in a brown light they will return,
one by one, toward sunset, glistening.
When they return, they will not return.
They will not be the same.

As I love you leaning down on you,
I feel the load I am you feel is me.
So the night blows. September passes.
The bay narrows by an inch of silt,
invisible to passing tenders night or day.
Debris goes by, waste hardens, fishes die.
The scene turns bare and freezes—
loses heart and changes.

Only we two stay the same in loving
what we bear, what we contain.

NOVEMBER THROUGH A GIANT COPPER BEECH

This almost bare tree is racing
taut in the wind, leaves flaring,
jet fire fed by a hurrying
keen whistling bird, against

hundred-limbed elephant branches,
steadied in wrinkled gray molten
antediluvian skin,
wrapped tight to stay where it is.

Think of sheer endlessness, beauty
patient in form, forever
uncrumbled between time's nickering
teeth—oh brutal necessity!

Think of the still and the flowing—
Heraclitus's *everything passes,*
The one-eyed conviction against
the rockheaded *everything dozes.*

On this bleary white afternoon,
are there fires lip up in heaven
against such faking of quickness
and light, such windy discoursing?

While November numbly collapses,
this beech tree, heavy as death
on the lawn, braces for throat-
cutting ice, bandaging snow.

BODEGA, GOODBYE

The wind is not right today.
It mocks the ancientness of beams
upholding this loose porch
that has shaded us all summer.
It makes the old porch shudder
and the termite dirt
leak down, down-down.

The wind fusses and blows wrong.
It makes the baby cranky
who should be sleeping in mild air
out of sun's reach on the crooked porch
by the half-gone wooden railing
where a smoked-out hornet's nest
lines the eaves like false teeth.

Night, and the wind still heaves
and gulps, and flaps the shades.
A nightbird cries as though
nothing had ever lain so still
as boulders in the moonlit field.
I turn over in my sleep
like a basket of broken bones.

SURVIVALS

TÊTE-À-TÊTE

Lifting his slowly trickling jaws
from whip-laced roadside grass,
the horse creased back a thighlong neck
in time to see me driven past,
an amputated head
framed by auto glass.

But was he really seeing me,
before he sank his eggplant head
to graze again, or the steel green car
that made his stare look drunk,
as though a bolting tree trunk
had kicked some memory ajar?

GLAD DAY
(after the Blake engraving)

I miss the Stone Age man who came last night.
Fierce and naked as he was, a gentle
inwardness clothed him; he was more at home
within my doors than I. You wouldn't say
he was the spit-and-image of anyone you knew,
or at a glance surmise his fix or fate.

No righteousness upheld his fleshy nose.
No analytic wrinkle pinched his forehead.

No clever practicality clenched his jaws.
Cheerfully he lit a fire and browned
the staring doe he'd killed and worn all day
walking through the burning sands alone.

"Let's eat!" I cried. Soon as the meal was done
he went—like that. When the dawn came up to drown
my sleeplessness, I rose and razed the house.
Refreshed before the ashes, I found these words
like honey on my tongue: "A new house is
abuilding on the underbelly of the world."

THE ISLAND

I

Hurt was the first language his heart heard.
Nothing human but was alien to him.
Words dropped pebbles through stone ears.
Eyes hardened the actual daylight, his prison.
Leaves' life tingled more than any hunger:
in autumn falling came their consummation,
fiery finales more baffling and sadder
for his not knowing what growing ate them.
A dry weeping swept his emptiness.

Come pale spring, again the weary growing.
Meeting and mating, mute light on tree trunks.

Over shell shucks the warm worm crawling.
Bullet-tipped boughs, leathery they lunge.
Mouths open eyes, new flesh moves old blood.
A swoop out of sleep, and the small prey cringes.
What says the rock to the rusty lichen, its hood?
In the sun you are good, but the coldness lingers.
Rain rots the fungi, nibbled by ants.

II

Summer came to watch from his shack
on the land-tip gray garbage-drenched waters,
gay buoys bobble, clean crafts idle
in the boulder-packed harbor,
rope-looped spiles creak to the backwash,
give and take, tauten and grate,
slip and slack, gurgle salt-heavy,
then bleaching, inhale, till each grim crack
fills with the whiff of an absent sea.

And always the oils, their main force colored
and spent, straggle unheeded, unfused,
streak heavily over the baywater's back.
Used, now a refuse listless as shells
the gulls leave blanching, upturned on rocks,
the life taken out: like orphans of death
still lifting on currents, in light, they mimic
the life they led, fueling the powering
motions of bodies their bodies once fed.

III

The hardened beach winked crystal, stung
and clawed again; foam clung gray
and trembled: some thin breeze compelled.
Half shells smooth as pearl were drier
than the sand, an eddied feather stilled.
Gold brow to glinting nails alert,
loose light spiralling her ears, her hair,
she bent and stared. The moment ended,
seas crashed his wish again, again.

His love fell through the spoiling summer:
a drooping wing down spiralling
amid the glinting silences
fell curling in glistening daylong forests;
like a smoke burrowing in crowded loneness,
all sound murdering, love's yearning
touched a small parched wing, and smokeless
burst aflame, and soundless fired
all his days of separate grownness.

IV

Death shares him with the night.
The broken eyes of three o'clock,
outraged, divide the writing
from the envelope pressed on
by the missing one; its happy
share inscribed, then sealed, then opened,

to be read by him alone,
lapses in estrangement on the table
till morning empties it in aftermath.

This is the room with books and chairs
that waits inaudibly; what does
the silence not-a-silence ask?
It asks the breath, the useful eyes
that scan it uselessly, what lives.
It asks to be, and not be listened
to; unmoved, unused, unkept,
waiting and awaited,
it begins an aftermath.

What knocks behind the sash knows this,
knows what least there is to know, to be.
Always he craves to enter, knowing,
as he did this room tonight, waiting
to begin the waiting afterward,
sharing—safe, estranged—the silence
of a room, an envelope,
a feeble knocking at the sash,
shared past death beyond the aftermath.

V

That lingering September before
the forest kneeled and died
under the giant equinoctial,
he slid down the shaly incline

past the shack to find the inmost
covered woods, but a moment's
turning backward glance
beheld the up and coming dawn
trifling through the empty shack.

And seen as from its risen eye,
the stir of himself through a whirlpool of air
sucked a hawk backward and down; lithe waters
caught fire, wild weather went whirling the five
o'clock sun around; a decade of seaweed
split open a boulder the burning high tide
gulped down; in the hawk's high lingering stare
the spell of himself, shuttered by boughs,
became a fallen feather of sound.

VI

In the weedy gardens of October,
rattling the dead leaves, the dead
come calling, bringing their dream,
an afternoon wine, through which he breathes
ethers of sun setting; they wreathe
round him the probing haze, and in him
press vineyards of their lost knowing.
A last late cry, a tired glow
is groping—clings, breathes up

And clears the silent wall—as faintly
in him unborn children creep,

crawl up to breathe this wine, this haze,
this seething dream of almost knowing.
Who if not they, borrowing
his being—the dead alive,
the unborn living—reach out,
almost bestow him, unwished
cradles and small crude tombs?

VII

The voice of winter cleared, then muffled,
then weighed the snaking path clean down to shale,
then ground it down to ruts and rock,
then paused and shifted like a guest
before a door who would be off
before he had been in, though knowing
all awaited him and that
the feast would not begin until
he thundered in and sat him down inside.

VIII

Now to become his early winter death,
heart's drone silenced there,
wind's tongue frozen sickling grass,
in summer turned about;
now to become his monument alone,
tethered there unread,

and by a thousand mornings
riffled through, unbroken stand;
now to become his own soiled hands,

Limp after tasks, humped fashioners,
destroyers of the fall's
gold tasselings, companions
ill and well; now to be,
become and be again,
past now, past seeing,
welcome—to each swelling
sun, the grave indwelling
gatherer, he prayed.

THE WEATHER'S CRIMINAL

(*Fair*)
First low, slow, slowly and sure,
then faster, faster and higher,
until he is almost gliding,
all effort past,
the black eagle rises.
It is morning everywhere.

(*Fair and Cool*)
The traffic noises move
my garden's heavy headed snowballs

once or twice
before they come to rest again.

(Warm)
Behind the railing
in the garden
I lie dozing
while sunlight speaks
its purpose like
an agate ring
flashed across
the iron gratings.

(Sleet in May)
Patient for his cue,
he waits,
his smile in view,
to say the thing that hurts.

(Gusts Before Tornados)
The sun blows dust against his panes.
The dust that's blown is deadmen's bones.
He sweeps his rooms out every day.
He wipes his windows bright again.
Then the sun turns dusty gray.

(Rampageous River)
All heart, no head, the bold man
lives alone,

and quarrels with the stone
he dines upon.

(Play of Early Sun and Clouds)
He slinks beneath the shadow
of his jury's fragmentary smile
and works his lips until
he gets them fixed
to his imagined understanding
of their total
soon to dawn
least possible compassion.

(Hurricane Eye)
He knows no end, he knows no start.
Utter life like utter death
refuses thought, refuses heart,
as fake illusion.
He's in collusion
with his life, of course,
but since he's bound to lose his breath,
he can't refuse
the fake illusion.
Though that way madness lies,
madness is no conclusion.

(Clearing)
All night by river falling
I hear the tumbling of frogs,
the chink of glinting stones,

the shift of broken branches
in their earthworn language
stalled, then racing on,
all flowing, going down,
no longer separate things
but meshing, taken in
the river's smoothing hand
and guided, lifted, driven
into the mashing sea.

(Doldrums)
We sat in the lamplight's quiet
estimation of
our wavering unanswered
fire, one moment in
his living brimful glass
in which each of us
contained it, each as yet
untouched, unbroken, asking
—Who will drink me if
we do not drink each other?
And neither of us stirred.

(Unsettled)
In gray quiet air the waiting
of the sky to fall
and the bony land beneath
to take whatever drops,
the rain, the leaf, the bird,
the hidden fire stone

that lies there momently
in the posture of a fallen thing,
to melt, dissolve,
freed of itself, and each
to be received forever
by this earth that takes,
folds everything received
slowly to itself
as vagrant flesh
of its accomplishing
and unforbidden self.

(Frost)
The sunlight owes December
a tolerable afternoon
for a cold wind I remember
crippling a day last June.

(Still Frost)
The year runs down to December,
old coldhearted detractor—
"Life is the fee you must pay
all at a blow in the end."
Waking too early in darkness
I hear this endlessly spoken.

(Winter)
Outside, great heights of crooked oaks
sweating under muffs of snow.

Inside, ash-surrendering logs
done with weather long ago.

(Winter King)
Towards cockcrow, when the inexhaustible poor
lay down and slept, some paid eye-witnesses,
just for the record, detailed an expiration.
They said the howling ceased, a calm descended,
a groggy soldier rose and walked off stiffly
in a borrowed coat. The hill began to shapen
where the stripped and cornered victim crept,
just as, from his riddled sides, a glory broke
and blazed. It shook, amazing and amazed—
as if enraged, as if it would not die.

THE FURNACE

News wrenched from the burning walls
  of the birth and bawling
    of infants contained
  to their toes, their billions
    of waving fingers;

News of revival, new presences
  under the sun
    and running the earth

   until they bounce
     surprised in our hands;

News broken slowly—it takes
such a time to reach
   the tips of our knowledge—
hooded, encroaching
   like flame to consume us;

News threaded into us till
we are fused to the children
   grown to our knowledge,
we see ourselves seen,
   tired and turning:

Who built the furnace? Who lit
the fire? Who led
   the billions full-blooded,
brainy and sheep-eyed
   into the flames?

The damper clinks in the hot stack,
the furnace is roaring,
   trembling we blink
and turn over, when *smash!*
   the news is another's:

   We are the flames.

IT CANNOT BE IT IS

Something moves that cannot be itself
Moves or is moved. Sullenly. A sluggish stream.

A garden winds among the densest rock.
Descends into a closure choked with weeds.

Something cannot be itself that spreads to feed.
Bucks. Then balks. Is almost broken.
Lashes out again and makes a scene.

A fallen body locked by stifled screams
Diminishes. Is frozen in a dream.

The winter world turns green. Soon summer twirls
Its canes of light across a darkening ravine.

It slides between and will not be itself.
No motive. No excuse. All license and expense.

Glittering it purls through living ooze.
As if to ask the mind to pocket it.
Without a thought. Companioned in complicity.

What can we call it? It grates and grinds. It burdens time.
It macerates. Grows fat. And famishes.

We sometimes hear a mewling in the night.
An infant dies. A cat is born. Bodies
In their heat that hammer on till dawn.

It rears. It lusts to swallow all that scene.
It moves to grasp a bellyful and burst.
Then shuffle off unseen.

God its name is
Pain its name is Pain its name is Pain

FOR C.

It came, a sudden comfort, soft, low-lying,
then like a fog half lifting, half still recumbent,
the shifting light shoots through,
a bolt of mindfulness awakened,
a breakthrough risen, quivering
with the first clear wording
of an answer to so dim a question
it seemed almost untrue—
the day when all at once you came in view.

WIFE

Woman, part flesh part salt,
under the immense blue
sun-blaring cause, see her

turning to the fire-fastened city,
her husband's warning cry
just dying on the molten air,

and she, drab wife bundled
in a prophecy,
that moment frozen, burning,

turning taller than
all her godstruck kin
breathless for the blessèd ark,

the curse of all her kind
wishing backward to
the lavish lurid safeties,

from puffing on those plains,
those horrid distances
of cold command.

MY LOVE IS ASLEEP

My love is asleep.
Whips of the grass
will not harm her.
Stones in the creek
will not bother to roll.
Hours will pass

and she will not hear
the crickets that crisp
their legs in the air.

But why does my heart
go suddenly cold?
Does she see how the crows
crowd into the sun?
Does she see how the shadows
thicken the trees?
I must waken my love
before she grows old
and heavy as stone.

WHAT CHANGES, MY LOVE

What changes, my love,
is the sunlight that slips
and shutters your smile for the night.

What rages, my love,
is the night wind that grips
and slackens your hand on my heart.

What tames me, my love,
is your smile that alights
and raises the roof of the day.

What stays me, my love,
is your hand dripping honey
out of my skinflint heart.

DEATH WITH ITS CUP OF HOPEFULNESS

Death with its cup of hopefulness
needs nourishment
but won't be fed by leftovers—
tired grief,
bewilderment of life's exhaust.
It moves in straight
to query your averted eyes,
turns out its hands,
looks past, then shuffles back,
fading in the shadows,
to wait again until
you find the food to share with it,
the daily take from your bleak bowl
lifted to your lips.

UNLESS LOVE DIE

Here tiny grave lights
and the shadow's ministry of fire

conspire briefly in the dark
to frame a wordless house.

All lies prone, vein-fed by dark,
till manhope starts the dayplay up,
till morning come and sting
the spectacle awake.

As all things wax before they wake,
as all things grow to be their fate,
the little night lights chatter,
Here you will rise, unless love die.

PASSING

>When hope dies, the straps that saddle us to time
>become undone, and we sit alone in space
>as in a place that can no longer hold us:
>not wishing yet to stir,
>we sit as though still held there,
>patiently, by nothing but our weight,
>yet with the weight itself no longer there,
>until the loss becomes a giddiness
>and we imagine movement is a falling,
>a lumping pratfall, a spraddling
>of diminished form on earth
>waiting to be gone.

From this we wake into another form
still wet with shaping, a form
as of another being never yet imagined,
and from this we view
the carcass of our former self:
as in a dream that says goodbye
to everything most intimately known,
briefly, quietly, without a qualm.
And when we rise, the waves of nothingness
beat and pull the topmost shore away.
Clearly gone, without a trace,
we are no longer there.

NOW, BEFORE THE END, I THINK

Now, before the end, I think
of how it was when we began:
in holding hands before we knew
each other, in touch there was the silent
awe of what we soon would know
in knowing one another later,
as though to heal the wounds that words
would cause before they were inflicted.

Now, wordless again, you reach to hold
my hand as if to say in silence,
it is healed, we touch, we are together.

We have heard the end, drifting
to the brink of a new silence,
holding hands in awe of being
now together, this moment, now,
now before we part forever.

NOW, MY USEFULNESS OVER

Now, my usefulness over,
the weight of your death
in a handful of ashes
drags at my mind.

My need is the lamp snuffed out
by your absence, and silence
all I have given
my mind to believe.

From ashes I carry you back
to your handsome warm fullness
and alight in a blackness
of time with the burden.

Turning I find myself emptied,
rifled of you and, cored
of my meaning, dumped
in a boneless sack.

Now stuck in my skin to wear,
minded over forever,
is this cruel and absolute
jewel of your life.

THE GAZABOS: FORTY-ONE POEMS

HAPPENING

Behind me the house was asleep.
I could hear it relax and breathe,
Tied to its summer thick hill.
A bird or a chipmunk scraped
Through the eaves or a hollow hand
Roamed in its paintless hide,
Tinkled a pane in the upper storey
While I walked and the house
Slept on. And it breathed,
I know, because it was then
The highest perturbable trees
Shook down a wind like a lash,
The road fell down a ravine,
And all that wide blue summer
Grew narrow and turned on itself
Like a fan. When I turned, the house
Had turned its face, gray as a man's.

ISLAND STORM

All morning in the woods I heard the bushes choke
   Among dead boughs that creaked and groaned,
And no other murmur than the flurry of live prey
   Grappling in the wind's slow teeth.

A starling toppled near the river-run, black
  As stone. A garter snake shivered
Up a root and instantly turned brown. It began
  On such a day prophets used
To rave about—"Stiff-necked mankind, remember
  Sodom and God's frown!" Through miles
Of tensing acreage only two eyes peeped when it
  Came down. The road became a falls
Where hubbubs fell to foam across a glazed surrendering
  Of channelled stone. In the hollow beat
Of some annihilating warmth, tumorous old stumps
  Were ground to muck. "Will it be day
Again?" I heard the brittle windows ask the lightning
  Flash, and tremble three full hours
As it spoke. Often, while the sea coughed distantly,
  Infamous last words of misanthropes
Ransacked my brain for counter-prayers. Below the eaves,
  Crackling like a greasy frying
Pan, only a floral lampshade quavered hope.

When at last the silence trickled in, I found
  The fungi like great plastered wounds,
The stupefying sweetness everywhere. And when
  The weather turned gigantically
And padded off, I found the world it left nearby:
  On the bloated attic floor
Two drowned mice; through the skylight, one fir
  Permanently bowed; above the flooded
Garden, the first fierce dart of an exploratory crow.

SPEECH

In the weedy gardens of October, rattling
the dead leaves, the dead come calling,
bringing their dream:
an afternoon wine through which
we breathe ethers of sun setting.

They wreathe round us the probing haze
and in us press vineyards of their
lost knowing: a last
late cry, a tired glow
is groping, clings, breathes up and clears

The silent wall as faintly in us
unborn children creep,
crawl up to breathe
this wine, this haze, this seeth–
ing dream of almost knowing.

Who if not they, borrowing our being—
the dead alive, the unborn
living—reach out,
almost bestow us, unwished
cradles and small crude tombs?

QUEST

Always when I see Italian marble
and great burnished mahogany sitting quiet
and ruthless in the indulgence of five centuries,

always I ask whose is the skull
set in jewels grinning there in shadow
who thrust all this from him feverishly

as the white dove flew nimbly from the mouth
and the feathers made great onslaughts
against the mind, loosening, flattening himself,

to dive into the eye of the needle.

THE TALL TOMS

All told the gray world
sponges hopelessly on swift
tall Toms, fliers in the
howling highways, scorchers
of the lush long countries.

Hats on or off they
head through glass,
through bowls of
winter roses, through
women hard as diamonds.

Floods and crosses
kiss their shoes, and
trolleys late for work
pray like snails till
sirens swill the streets.

Their failure is success
in the eye highballing
white and black, and if
they end, even grim lids in
grass plots ponder over them.

AS A GREAT PRINCE

    As a great prince after the hunt comes
Stomping through the antlered spear-hung hall
Of his over-nourished leisure, flopping his weight
    Of rich self-certitude to dream in thick
    Bearskin the teasing horror of a beast
Outstaring axe blows, questioning the onslaught,
In immortal posture gazing and uncaught,

    So we inhabit a drowsy movie dark,
Amid love's trophies deliberating self-content,
Moist anticipants of the overplayed crescendo
    Clutching the smoking guns of pleasure,

    Till suddenly blond beast removes a robe
    And pulsing reel relaxes to a still
    Of smiling passion frozen in our death of will.

MAY 1945

    Spring's great wafer caked in the mouth.

    One-legged beggars hopped out of cellars
    Reeking of dressings and brass.

    Blue-lipped Rhine maidens whining like sheep
    Slowly uncrossed their thighs.

    Numb in the eyes Faustus went down
    Nuzzling the conqueror's heel.

    The corpses of Europe lay back in their char.

JANE RETREAT

    Jane Retreat falls stark asleep
    In her large brown-headed shoulders.

The rest of her starts
Like fish half alive
Under the fumbling dark.

Where will the fire be found
To pilot the dark on Jane half awake?

O Jane Retreat
With your fish in my arms
Tugging through half the night:

If only someone would crawl through my veins
To tear out your shoulders and head!

ANCESTORS

On the slouch-roofed porches of the green
Hotel, guests from rock-ribbed centuries
Sit erect, playing at regrets;
Sympathies like ashen chessmen pass
From hand to hand and crumble in their cold
And queasy grasp, until to rockers creaking
Like the chomp of axes ghostly waiters
Come with shawls and razor smiles to cut
Them off, neck by windy neck.
                                       And where
Boards sigh that headlong enterprise, my mother,

Choking, rocks an empty cradle; all
Birds impersonate my granny's voice,
And dust-enshrouded mosses, like my grandpa,
Sway in lost soliloquies of prayer.

FOR AN IMMIGRANT GRANDMOTHER

She sat for an age at the window with glances that threw
Pennies of pity at collarless beggars, and cripples
Who crawled like crabs from gutter to curb rippled
The geese in the bag of her hunched-over flesh. But you
Always could tell by her murmur for heaven to witness
When neighborhood children like sparrows hopped in
    distress
To catch from the hand of the baker his three-day-old
    bread.

Yet she danced with a hint of the hips and a lilt of the
    head,
And the savor of turbans and princes and spices welled
From her smile like a promise of Turkish delights
    withheld;
For her heart was a mediterranean cradling the earth
With wishes that tumbled like fish and golden sea fairs

Where pirates were drowned and angels were spared by
    her prayers,
Till she slipped unaware on the edge of a sigh to her
    death.

GRAMMARIAN THUMBING AN OLD TEXT

Ribbons, bracelets drop, hose wrinkles down.
    (God showed this lady to be brave.)
Tugged at, untied, stripped clean from heel to crown
    (God told this lady to behave),
Until, thrust open like a stack of sheaves
    (God bound this lady to be moved),
In darkness plunged, she labors to a scream.
    (God owed this lady to be loved.)

Who fails to rise and harrow, folds greatness in.
    New flesh waits to make the old bones sing,
Complete two separate bloods in one sweet wailing.

    Say this hallowed lady rounds our dream
Forever; but God, before you thrust her altarward,
    Say, is she Eve or Queen—or Babylon abhorred?

LEASE AND LOSS

Fear of all fineness falling off, the one
Dream already dreamt that cannot be
Revisited the rising moment when
We turn to the familiar patience of a roof
And find the ruin, the lintel lapsing, death's
Fingers in the beams—

These are the lush last hours when gardens
Talk to thrushes what we cannot hear
And they obey, repeat the summons clearly,
And a sudden tree in all its hair quickens
Till nothing matters but that gone vibration
In its slowing hair.

Four seasons, a common year of fables ends.
Our stare is grass. The clacking audits
Of those days whirl back to stack the loss as
Not we but gardens turn proprietory
To the dim need of rooting longer
Something almost past.

The gardens aren't ours who were loaned
And ownerless. By hours clipped and thrown
To the last quick speech, to the blown
Word that touched the thrush, to the cold
Puff that rustled in the tree's crown,
Deprived, possessed, we go.

THE MARRIAGE

She turned her golden elbows in
And laughed. The pond was scattered. One
Leaf idly looping, gray side up,
Stuck to her fluent petticoat.

I said it was her weather's badge
That shivered now. A fish flashed.
It silvered all her teeth as I
Explored my shadow in her eyes.

That moment the tree, bird-loaded, broke
Into a cloud. When we awoke,
Her smile in mine and thigh to thigh,
The yellow pond involved the sky.

OUTER DRIVE

Heat of nightfall, and the heave and start,
Beside a quivering sleek trolley on the track,
Of a sudden snub-cabbed truck, trailerless,
Intense; like a bullhead bodiless it rockets
Just grazing past the green tan flank
Of the wincing public car, lit up with heads
Featured in the window squares, going
Straight and ironbound, by safety islands,
Down the flickering neon evening, home—

While the deathless disembodied bullhead of a truck
Escapes: past stoplights raging, headlights steaming,
Rips through city limits, eating, eating,
Eating all the highway up to Albany.

W
A
L
WHITMAN
Prophet of the body's
roving magnitude, he still
commands a hope elusive as the Jewish
savior—not dying, not yet born, but always
imminent: coming in a blaze one sunny afternoon,
defying winter; to everyone's distinct advantage, then going on
to Eden, half sham, half hearsay, like California or Miami golden.
All his life was squandered
in his poverty when he became
the body's prime reunionist, bankrupt
exploiter, from early middle age, of the nation's
largest unexploited enterprise—baggy, queer,
a Johnny Appleseed freely planting selve's the future mashes
into commonplaces, lops off as flourishes, an unweaned appetite.
Yet who can shape his mouth's
beard brimming bubble, that violent honey
sound? Afterwards they just blew hard,
Tarzans hamming through the swampy lots.
His patent, never filed, was being man quixotically
alive against the hoax of sin & dying. Paradise is now.
America, whose greatest war was civil, must be born from Abel's wound

        & Cain be welcomed home
          by Adam—Father Abraham
           opening his blood to continents,
   all armies, lovers, tramps. A time for heroes, but
the captains, shot or dowdy, died. (Had old Abe really smiled
& tipped his hat or had he merely grimaced?) Ulysses, finished, promptly
sighed & chomped cigars & toured the capitals. The people yea'd & shambled
            to the greatest fortunes
              made, while he conveyed the lippy
                cop, the whistling streetcar man, the ferry
                  pilot billowing upon the apron of his praise.
                Nakedly at last he flailed his own paralysis
with mud & flesh-brush. A man, all men himself alone, a rugged blue-
eyed testament, his looks in Brady's lens are calm with after-rages.
                    "The real war
                      will never get
                        in the books."
                      Below the ragged
                        line   he   signed
                          his chummy name.

THE GAZABOS

    I saw them dancing,
the gazabos, apes of joy, swains of
their pocket mirrors, to each a world:
    a dancing, a gallumphing, a guzzling
      of themselves.

    They yapped, they cooed,
they flapped their feet and winked grimaces
into grins. They rapped their knuckles on
    their teeth and bled and licked
      the blood like honey.

    Turning the corner
to my street, I spat on each
gazabo as they came. They loved it,
    they could barely keep
      from following.

    I had to beat
them off with barbed wire switches
ripped from neighbors' fences on
    the way. I escaped
      only when

      they paused to smear
their bodies with their trickly wounds,
streaming welted faces ogle-
    laughing in the mirrors
      sideways.

   Why is it now,
safe in my lacquered room, cradled
in my black, spoon-shaped easy
   chair, the whitest sheet
     of paper on

     my knees, I cannot
write a word? I read their eyes,
I taste their wounds. Do they live
   because they simply
     cannot die?

     Friends, multi-
tudes, oh lifelong shadows: are
you my filth, my worn out longings,
   my poems that dog me
     till I die?

THE MORAL CIRCUS

LAST ACT

A skilled dissembler, bound stock-still behind
   The wine-dark curtains, reassembles
Your impossible mischance. The playhouse lights
   Are doused, the last butt hastily
Crushed out. Mercilessly patient they
   Await the gory disentanglement.

How can the beggar really be a lord?
   The bawdy goat, his vengeful brother?
This much-handled girl in black, his lawful
   Wife? Whose priest is this, dry index
And defamer of the longest doubt, invokes the voice
   Of whom? Most greedy now your image

Bleeds and flares. Defy the act! Deny
   The self! while all machines, the pulse,
The past, the play's derisive twist of plot
   Collapse, and all he sees is you,
Your famished desperation. Drenched in amber
   His great head imbibes your agony

Until a stricken patron staggers up the aisle—
   A would-be worshipper deceived.
Fathoming the grave enchantment, he enacts
   Not you, your last diffuse articulation.
He clambers dazzling to the welcome crime,
   A rapture of himself, and hovers where

It only seems miraculous to die. Then broken,
   Drained of you, is quickly haloed.
The king is dead! The bleeding actor lies.
   Wet-eyed, wild, they rise. The mended
Body bursts the curtains wide, and arches
   On their synchronous ovation.

HAMLET

Ingenious, young, and forever captain
Of the art enlivening the personal debate,
You live to plague the long-trenched certainties
Of middle age, the platitudes of honored
Ripeness, and like a bitter tide wash on
The firmly anchored properties of lust.

Polonius in his apothegm is privy
To your rage. Behind the trembling arras
His sad witness is the planted effigy
Of some plot to bash your reason in,
Unhinge revenge, misguide the stubborn poniard
Craving toward its fearful fleshy home.

The flesh is all to everyone, and yet
A commonplace as cheap as swelling snow—
Unless, a lurid bait, it slip the sleeper
Into warm-pressed sheets to meet his nude

Full-breasted, thigh-entwining mate:
Ophelia's mother-masked, incestuous hoax.

But far beyond that play-enchanted hall
Of killing joys and slapstick horror roles,
The lip-loud girls, the raffish serving boys,
Glow arrows of inflamed conceits toward goals
Of intellect past cudgeling, where curseless
Fathers sup from Plato's golden bowl.

O there to rise with power to divine
The tear from torrents of delayed lament,
And wear the motley diamond of the self
On all one was and is, against the death
Of speech, the shrivelling skin, and be
Sermon on the mount of one's own requiem.

THE MORAL CIRCUS

In the spangled tent where the clowns jump high
The lights went out, and even the sky.
They were playing night with bears and drums,
But the fat lady went on eating plums.

I had just sauntered in on my only day off
To hear the Commandments given by a dwarf

Perched on a pole in the stratosphere.
When lightening came we all began to cheer.

When nothing happened, the silence grew.
You couldn't even hear the fat lady chew.
Bears stopped rolling, clowns lay flat,
The dwarf didn't budge from where he sat.

Feeling floored and fleeced and irked,
I shouted, "Give us the Law!" And it worked.
As everybody left who'd come in on passes
The falling dwarf handed me his glasses.

I was putting them on with a thousand amens
When ten blind clowns walked through the lens.
They sneered, "Of course nobody would stay.
You should be alone on your holiday."

"DO YOU LOVE ME?"

Inside the candid night blue room
A shift is sounded—"Do you love me?"—
As a body crunches down the street
Against the first lighting of the frosted
Lamppost. Her dying sigh denies
The quiet settling idly on
His polished shoe. One blunt toe

Gleams back a flawless eye at him
As he dangles from the sigh.

"Tell me, do you love me?" He is caught
Quick as a fish's lip. Secretly
His tongue darts up to test for bleeding.
Does a hooked fish breath blood before
Pure air drowns it? Fool! What is
This living bait you snatch at? his slumped
Body asks, past guilt, believing
In its fix. If he turns to greet
Her eyes, he is chucked out dry.

He tastes his words like grit. "As
I love myself—sometimes," he tries.
Silver sugar bells he stole one Christmas
Somehow defame him now. No reply.
Abjectness battens on her questions.
He dreams of knives surviving wounds,
Innocent of bloody issues:
Which the victim, which the quickened
Instrument that sticks and steals away?

His eyes' amazing clarity defies
The misted window, finds the sole
Pedestrian, a bundled blob, to envy
At the farthest lamppost near the crossing.
Blue frost blackens when the traffic
Blots that last survivor out.
Abandoned to his doubt, the street

Retreats, distills the pulsing silence.
The killer fades into his crime.

"Then it's all a lie!" she shouts.
He thrashes free upon the elemental
Ground and flings the bait straight back:
"I've never denied it yet!" But is it
His lie merely to find out? For when
She tears her heavy grievance out
And mounts the stairs to cry, surprised,
He feels his bubbling neck, the head
Detached and following the bait above.

Outside it hails true diamonds. Shadows
Trickle down the page flattened
On his lap. Unhooked, he floats
Into his own decapitated calm.
But whose mild unpunishable eyes
Are nibbling at the open book?
Unclenched, his humped up body will
Soon rise to switch on, gloating in
The dark, the flagrant reading light.

DITTY TO HIS LOVE

If you need me
Call the sea.
I'll not come harrowing
Your willowy white shore.
I will keep

Shipwrecks deep,
Withhold my swarming green-eyed reach
From feathery privacies of beach.

If you need the sea
Call for me.
I will tumble from the stars
As gently as anemones.
For your sake
I will break
My whale hoarse voice, and round your cove
Will lace my teeth in pearls of love.

But if you run
For wind or sun
Instead of me, I'll litter your hair
With jittery crabs and eels,
With barnacle combs
And dead men's bones,
And woo me another wench of a shore
As seas, my pet, have done before.

FIRST MORNING

Nude and tall the morning sang
The clammy beach, the rustling foam;
Striped green and tan
The morning swam
The rusting air, the ravelling sand.

Mists on rocks that hung in flame
The salt clear morning sprang beyond;
Sprained gulls in twins
Came lazying
To pin their smoky shadows down.

Still the morning young and gold
Among the fish devouring shoals
Sang out the old
Imprisoned song
Of the madcap water walls.

Helmeted the sun arose
To spear the corpse of blue and cold;
Among the coves
It rang and flowed;
The morning shuddered once and stalled.

Shells breathed our a mossy smell,
Starfish curled in air like tinsel;
The morning sprawled,
The gulls applauded,
The rocks the sun swung on said Peaceful.

Small and white the morning sailed,
A brutal fleck of fierce lipped sea,
Upon the sun
Whose bursting vein's
First song will be—come yesterday.